Into the CLOUD

BECOMING GOD'S SPOKESMAN

ERIC WILLIAM GILMOUR

FOREWORD BY TONY KEMP

First Printing: August 2014
14 15 16 17 18 19 20   10 9 8 7 6 5 4 3 2
Printed in the United States of America

<u>DEDICATION</u>

To my wife, Brooke, and my two children, Madison Tate and Lia Ashlyn, without whom this short life would be most lacking in the greatest joys and pleasures. I love you all more than anything that could ever be put into print. 943

Eric W. Gilmour

ACKNOWLEDGMENTS

I would like to express my gratitude to the many people who saw me through this book; to all those who provided support, talked things over, read, wrote, offered comments, allowed me to quote their remarks and assisted in the editing, proofreading and design.

I would like to thank my lovely wife Brooke, who has stood by my side as my greatest friend and confidant. You are the love of my life and my sweet soul mate. Thank you for enabling me to get away for extended periods of time to sit in the sweet presence of Jesus, without which none of this material would have been experienced, let alone penned. I want to thank my dear friend and hero, Daniel Kolenda who has supported and encouraged me to continue to fulfill the call of God on my life. *Christ for all Nations,* thank you for the support and friendship through the years. I also would like to thank the Sonship International partners, in particular, my grandparents Jack and Millie Ramos for your prayers and support, Neal and Judie Wise, faithful Joy Twitty and Christiana Lacroix, Evangelist Bernie Moore, Michael Dow of the Burning Ones, sweet Lynn Martin and her dear husband Michael Martin who has gone on to be with Jesus, Howard and Carol Merricks standing by our side in the advancement of the gospel in the earth, Andrew and Jocelyn Lamb who have believed in us, Scott and Jackie Howe whose friendship and ministry helped us tremendously throughout our lives and the launch of Sonship International. Thank you to all our partners who have prayed and stood by us from the beginning.

I would like to thank Tony Kemp for writing the foreword to this work and for his father-like wisdom to me over the last few years. Also, thank you to my dear friend David Popovici whose meekness and militancy constantly sobers my spirit — there is no one like you. Thanks also to Brian Guerin and Michael Koulianos for true covenant love and support — you guys are the eagles of the earth.

I extend my gratitude to Jim McMahel and Christiana Lacroix for helping me in the process of selection and editing. Thanks to Wally F. Gilmour, my Dad, who has always been my number one fan. Also, Deborah Gilmour my Mother who has been the most hidden foundational figure of my physical and spiritual life, I wish I could utter an endless I love you.

Thanks to Wally E. Gilmour, my big brother, who has been by my side in all the phases of my life, love you bro. To my sister, Shalisa Kelly, I know things haven't been like we thought they would through the years, but I love you, "live it well." Thank you to all who have purchased and commented on my books *BURN* and *UNION*, your kind encouragement has inspired me.

Last and not least: I beg forgiveness of all those who have been with me over the course of the years and whose names I have failed to mention.

Now unto the King eternal, immortal, invisible the only true and wise God – You are the air of my soul, my food and my drink, my strength and my pleasure. To You, and only You, be all glory, honor and praise — Great Lamb of God, The Flame of Heaven and The One And Only Sovereign God.

Table of Contents

FOREWORD

There are secrets to experiencing the satisfaction of the Spirit by eating the Bread of Life (Jesus), and as a holy result, enjoying a full fellowship with the Father in the Cloud of the presence. In the pages of this book, Eric reveals the ancient paths, the hidden keys that open doorways into a life that few have found, but many are seeking; a life lived in love and joy within the harmony of Heaven Himself.

Eric reveals that by dismissing reason and embracing the revelation of the Word, one discovers freedom from religion and ascends from earth into heaven itself to become one with the One.

The Hebrew song division 46:10 says you can "be still" to "know the I AM." By the practice of stillness, Eric teaches us to intimately and deeply come to know The I AM.

Through becoming synchronized with the Holy Spirit, we experience oneness with the One. For it is written, that he who is "joined to the LORD is one spirit." You cannot and will not become God, but you can walk in the Spirit (enter the cloud) to be transformed into the image and likeness of the One you worship – Jesus the Lord of Glory!

The revelation is that our life brings an impartation of The Life so that we may transmit that Life to others. Your highest hopes and fondest dreams are in the cloud! Enter the cloud and you will find that the God of all glory is waiting to meet you there! Put application to the revelation you are about to read and become one with the One, the Lord of glory!

TONY KEMP
Quincy, Illinois, March 2, 2014

INTRODUCTION

"We are writing about the Word of Life, Him..."
~1 John 1:1 AMP

In the midst of all the issues that theologians have supposed to be in existence at the time of John penning his first letter, John's antidotal subject is, "the Word of Life." As John the beloved revelator saw it, this communicative revelation of God that dispenses God's own substance into the human soul is prescribed as the recipients' all-encompassing remedy. No matter what the issues actually were, we are certain of this: the Word of Life — Jesus, the only begotten of the Father — is the only antidote.

Jesus is the communication, revelation and impartation of God's life. He is God's Word of life communicating God to men. Jesus, as the voice of God, is the revelation of God, and as the revelation of God, He is also the impartation of God. Jesus is not only "what God is saying;" He is God's expression: "now He has spoken to us in Son."[1] All God's speaking is inside of this living individual. We must seek to find Christ present in the depths of the scriptures, not merely as type and shadow, but as the living word, the present speaking of God.

John tells us that Jesus is, through communication, the revelation of God which imparts God into man. Witness Lee said, "God became man that He might dispense Himself into men." This great allocation is by the means of the Word of

Life, God's own communicative revelation. Revelation means the unveiling, the uncovering, or the disclosing of something. Jesus, who is God's speaking, reveals God to man. He is the communicative revealing of God. He is both the dispensing of God into the human soul and the divine means by which God dispenses Himself into us. God's chosen means of imparting Himself into man is communication; the reception of His Word. We are born again by the Living Word into a life that lives by the constant receiving of the Living Word.

With this understanding we turn our attention to the Word of Life as John's prescribed remedy for the issues surrounding the recipients of his letter. Many of the corrective issues and cautions in 1 John are easy to spot by the very content of the letter, all of which are remedied by the communication, revelation and impartation of God's life into men:

Lack of the joyful fellowship with God (1:3)
People walking in darkness claiming light (1:6)
People saying they have no sin (1:6)
Evidence of actual fellowship (2:4)
Love (2:11)
Love of the world (2:15)
Antichrists (2:18)
Abiding in Christ/the light of Christ's return (2:28)
Sin (3:5-7)
Hated by the world (3:13)
Confidence in prayer (3:22)
Antichrist/perfection of love at Judgment (4:17)
Protection (5:18)
Idols (5:21)

John chooses to expound upon the voice of God — His personal communication as a revelation and transmission of

Himself into the human soul — as the subject remedy to these issues: "we are writing to you concerning the Word of Life, Him..." It is this dispensing element into the human soul, the hearing of God, which changes men. The receptivity of God's voice is the most transformative phenomenon. In the beginning, when the world was "formless and void and darkness was over the face of the earth," what happened to bring form and substance and light to this dreadful condition? It was the speaking of God: "the Spirit of God hovered over the waters and God said..." In such a scene, God set before us His own pattern: God's work is God's speaking in the presence of God's Spirit. So it will be in your life as well. Light and clarity come from His voice in His presence. If you are formless and confused and seemingly void in life and purpose, it is the substance of God's voice that will deliver you. For God's communication gives us revelation, in which God performs impartation.

Let us continue this pattern in which the work of the Spirit and the revelation of Jesus are united. In John 14, we see the gift and work of the Holy Spirit described to us by Christ. In this work of the Spirit, verse 19 shows us that the Holy Spirit causes us to see Jesus when the world does not. By this vision of Him who is unseen we live, for even Moses endured seeing Him who is unseen. The Scriptures are clear that we look to Him and live.[2] Jesus says, "you will see me because I live, you will live also." This light, this vision, and this seeing has a threefold revelation.

You will know that I am in the Father. This is a revelation of Jesus, giving us an instantaneous understanding that Jesus is actually inside of the Father.

You will know that you are in Me. This is a revelation of the fact that those who believe have been absorbed into Christ, who is inside the Father.

And you will know that I am in you. This is a revelation that Christ is inside of you; this is the mystery of "Christ in you, the hope of glory." Paul said that God didn't just reveal His Son to Him but IN HIM.[3]

In this seeing is life, and in this life is revelation by which a man can be empowered to obey. The obedient one enters into deep love and union with God, and, according to verse 21, the love of the Father is also united with a revelation of Jesus. Jesus is the endless vision; Christ is the perpetual revelation. We can be assured that a person of great revelation is one greatly loved by the Father, and that one who is in love with God possess great revelation of God. Verse 23 unites the revelation of Jesus with the Godhead abiding in us. Again, the dispensing of the Godhead into us is united with the revelation of Jesus, and that revelation is united with the production of obedience in life from looking unto Him (see verse 19). This is the ministry of the Holy Spirit to reveal Jesus, the Word of Life.

I write this book to inspire great respect and value for Word of Life. I write to inspire us to enter into His speaking, the means by which He is dispensed into the earth. Speech is the greatest way God dispenses Himself into the earth. Jesus is that speaking of God, for God is always testifying of His Son. God's endless pontification is Jesus Christ which He performs only by the breath of His own Spirit. This is how He gives life: "He who has the Son (His speaking) has life and He who has not the Son (His speaking) has not life." It is my personal belief that John delivers to us revelation of a higher quality than that of any other writer. He alone distinguishes Christ as the Word of God. He constantly refers to Him as light, life, love and fellowship, which are personally my favorite words, because they suggest so much to our understanding. Life: that animating source of existence that God Himself is; Light: that illuminating and blinding brilliance; Love: the selfless laying down of one's self for another; and Fellowship: the interactive divine exchange — this is mystical language. How often have you heard emphasized that following Jesus means direct contact with God? Has it been common for you to hear that we are to be illuminated and animated by God's own substance? Dear reader, I don't know what the core pursuit and passion of your life is, but I tell you that above all things, I want God to possess me. I salivate for it. I groan for it. I constantly think of it. I believe the words, "life", "light", "love" and "fellowship" to be the specific revelation to us from John and an indispensable factor to the authentic Christian life.

Christ is life. Christ is the Word of life. We must hear Him. Those who are most like Him are those who are most united with Him. Our union with Him, in this time, is only by His presence and His voice, the inseparable combination, for "the Word was with God." This verse forever settles the location of the Word: the Word is with God. To become God's spokesman we must enter into the cloud; that manifestation of God's presence in which God speaks. In John 12:41 the Scripture states, "These things Isaiah SAID BECAUSE HE SAW His glory, and spoke of Him." The impetus of a prophet's speaking is his seeing. His glorious encounter produced speech. The Word of Life is birthed in the glory. It is in the prophet's personal encounter with God, that He becomes God's communication to the world. Lifeless speech comes from believing that we have life apart from Him. So if we recognize that only what God says lives, then we will only say what He says. The prophet becomes his message. He does not prepare messages but speaks what has been spoken into him; he speaks what he himself has become. It was John the Baptist's delight in the Voice that made him a Voice.4

John 12:49 shows us that when God tells us what to say, this then becomes a commandment for us to obey…by speaking it. Jesus called the things that God told Him to say "a commandment." The word He uses here has to do with "that which is prescribed to someone by reason of their office." That thing that God gives to us is an order, a charge. To truly steward the speaking of God, we must look at Jesus. Jesus didn't just say that He speaks what the Father told Him but that He speaks what the Father told Him "*as* the Father told" Him. The only way to deliver the Word without subtraction or addition, and in the same spirit, is to become the speaking. I am afraid that many have heard the word and have spoken it but have failed to speak how the Father spoke. I submit to you that such a one has failed to swallow the Word. When God came to Ezekiel with the edible scroll, it forever settled what is in the heart of God for His spokesman to be. The edibility of the heavenly scroll reveals that the Scriptures are not confined to the lesson of the letter. The lesson of the letter can only lodge itself in the memory of man while the consumption of the scroll transforms the man into oneness with the Word.

I have written these chapters as I have heard from the Father while caught up in His presence. I have been fed and filled personally through these particular revelations from the Scriptures and now it is time for them to pass into others.

Lord, I pray that even though my pen is far inferior to the quality of the enduring classics, that You will have mercy, use these words to draw men into the cloud, speak into them, and teach them to become Your spokesmen in the earth.

I will close out this introduction with a quote from Bernard McGinn.

"Mysticism is the element in Christianity that seeks a heightened and transformative consciousness of God rooted in the Scriptures, not just historical, but a spiritual reading that rewrites the Bible within the heart, finding in the depths of the text a direct encounter with God that transforms the reader."
-Bernard McGinn

Eric William Gilmour
November 2013

---

1 Hebrews 1:2

2 Isaiah 45:22; The Raising of the Serpent as Christ in John chapter 33 Galatians 1:16

3 Galatians 1:16

4. 1 John:1:23, 29

Eric W. Gilmour

CHAPTER ONE

THE STILLNESS OF THE SOUL

"Can you imagine any greater thing than to have communion with God Himself and to be wholly absorbed by Him?"
-Evagrios of Pontus

"Stillness is the mother of prayer."
-John of Damascus

"Put a seal on your senses by stillness."
-Thalassios the Libyan

Stillness has three elements: "The first is freedom from the anxieties of life; the second is a clear conscience; the third is complete detachment, such that your thoughts no longer buzz around materialities. When you have acquired these things, sit down by yourself in a quiet place, out of the way of everyone, and close the door and withdraw your intellect from all worthless and transient things..."
-Symeon the New Theologian

THE STILLNESS OF THE SOUL

"(Martha) had a sister called Mary, who was seated at the Lord's feet, listening to His word. But Martha was distracted with all her preparations; and she came up to Him and said, "Lord, do You not care that my sister has left me to do all the serving alone? Then tell her to help me." But the Lord answered and said to her, "Martha, Martha, you are worried and bothered about so many things; but only one thing is necessary, for Mary has chosen the good part, which shall not be taken away from her."
~Luke 10:38-42 NASB

Since the activation of the New Covenant, purchased by the blood of Christ and installed in us by the presence of the Holy Spirit, the spiritual man can now enjoy direct interaction with God. This blissful life of union with the person of God brings the spiritual seeker into an increasing awareness, consciousness and experience of God. The internal disposition of the soul has everything to do with this experience, for experiential union with God has its roots in experiential fellowship with God. Contained in these five verses in the tenth chapter of Luke's gospel, exists what I believe to be the clearest practical picture of the choice that is ever and always before us: to live still in adoration or in scattered activity. We must ask ourselves, are our souls resting or are they restive?

CONTEMPLATIVE OR ACTIVE

Activity is our default disposition and must be daily suffocated with tranquil adoration. The mystical teachers and theologians throughout church history sought to find a balance between the "contemplative life" and the "active life." I do not believe that the issue is a matter of "activity" versus "contemplation."

Nor do I believe that the issue lies in finding the perfect ratio of how much "activity" we should be involved in or how much "contemplation" we should have in our lives. I submit to you that this thinking causes us to miss the whole point. God does not seek to make us servants only but rather desires that we receive His Spirit to make us His own children. Christ even responded to the spirit of religion that sought to kill Him (John 5:16-17) with the revelation of His union with God as Father. His Sonship was not a matter of credence or devotion but rather the very core of His existence.

My friend, this is what it means to be born again. We have been born of God, by His very own Spirit, not drafted into a maid service. This may not make much sense to the natural mind, but the servant works while the son simply is. "It is not a matter of doing but being," as John G. Lake stated so clearly one hundred years ago. Martha's service died with her but Mary herself became a message to all generations. Whatever Martha was specifically doing was not even worthy enough to be mentioned; it was so insignificant to Luke and to the Spirit of God, who moved him to write this gospel, that there is not even a description of her preparations "for the Lord." Simply put, Martha worked while Mary worshipped.

As we look at these two women we will see the most practical picture, painted by Luke's pen, concerning the stillness of the adoring life that *becomes* something, in contrast to the striving life that strains to *do* something. I pray that the remainder of this chapter on stillness would reveal to us that the issue is not a matter of contemplation verses activity but rather that God is after something so much greater than could ever have been explained through making such a division.

SISTERS

The first thing to note is that Martha and Mary are sisters. They are not distant cousins or friends, not acquaintances or business partners. They live together under the same roof, related and connected, yet distinctly different: Martha is a restive soul, scattered and spread thin while Mary is a soul that is still, at rest and attentive to Christ. Both of them welcome the presence of Christ, yet they respond to Him differently.

Have you felt Martha dart and hustle through your veins? She lives under the roof of your being, always there, ready to act, arrange and manipulate. Have you also sensed Mary's serene posture and attentive gaze upon Christ? I am sure you have felt both of these internal conditions. For they live together as sisters under one roof in which is the presence of Christ Himself. He is equally available to them, yet dissimilarly availed by them. Wherein lies this dissimilarity? Let us first look at Mary of Bethany, this eternally noteworthy individual.

MARY

1. Notice the very first thing written about Mary: "...who was seated..." Her position is representative of her disposition. She is not antsy or fidgety, but seated and at rest. She is not running and up on her feet but reposed on the floor. In being seated she is also low, symbolizing humility. She looks up to the Lord as He speaks and not down upon him in pride or even level with His eyes. Her example makes my heart sing, for she scandalizes everyone who loves the work of the Lord more than the Lord of the work.

2. She is not just still, resting and humble; she is "...at the Lord's feet..." in adoration. She is in the position of a

servant who washes her Master's feet, a worshipper who bows before and kisses the object of her affection.

3. The lowly, still, resting, adoring heart alone listens to His voice. Mary is "...listening to His word..." attentive to Him. She does not speak for she gazes upon and listens to Him, receiving into herself the very Word – Christ: His very own thinking patterns, His very own Spirit, and yes, His very own life; His words are Spirit and Life.[1]

Can you see her there restfully still, quietly adoring, humbly gazing and attentively soaking in every ounce of honey that drips from His lips? Oh Mary, you move my heart to look unto Jesus and simply rest in Him. Friends we must recognize that some men describe honey but Jesus dispenses honey. Our souls will long for human activity until they are finally blessed by the honey that drips from His lips.

MARTHA

Now let us turn our attention to Martha.

1. The very first thing noted about Martha is that she is "distracted..." Martha cannot concentrate upon the Lord, but rather is prevented from giving her full attention to the Lord and His words. She cannot hear Christ, for the clanking of the pots and pans, deafened by the sound of her own hustle and haste. The number one reason why Christians do not experience the presence of the Spirit of Christ inside them is because they are preoccupied and inattentive. Christ is no less present to Martha than he is to Mary, but Mary experiences Christ far beyond Martha. Nothing so distracts us from *being* like *doing*. Few things pull us

from a life of adoring Him like a life of working for Him.

2. Martha makes her own ministry unto the Lord instead of ministering to the Lord. The Scripture says that Martha was busy "with all her preparations...." Notice the source of the preparations. Her works do not originate in God, but rather herself. She operates under self-imposed labor and erroneous requirements, for after all, these are "*her* preparations." A life of activity makes its own ministry for the Lord while a life of adoration is a ministry unto the Lord.

3. "She comes up to him...." Notice, Martha's coming to the Lord, was motivated by her competitive and comparative eye; she was seeking aid for her own preparations. She did not come to Him for His own sake; her prayer had a foundation other than adoration, namely, self. Martha is always trying to get God to look at her circumstances instead of simply looking to Him. Oh, how much activity is done without looking at Jesus!

4. Martha's question to Christ baffles me every time I read it: "...Do you not care?" Consider who is the most caring being that will ever exist? Is it not God who left heaven and substituted His own life to save rebellious and sinful mockers through humiliation and torture? This exposes the fact that Martha had a distorted view of Christ, caused by her own lack of adoration. Here lies the root of all of our disfigured revelation of Christ, the core of any misunderstanding we might have of God: preoccupation and distraction in the soul. When an individual becomes too busy to look unto Jesus in worship and taste the honey from His lips, that

individual will end up saying, "God, do you not care?" Even in the presence of God, this individual will blame, misrepresent, and even misunderstand God's personality if he does not live a life of devotion in God's presence listening to His voice.

5. Martha turns the attention of God to Mary: "My sister..." This gives such clear evidence that in order to turn our eyes upon another person, we first have to take our eyes off Christ. Many ministries have been built by looking at other people's failures or errors, when the only real building of God is constructed upon a revelation of Jesus. Christ said in response to Peter's revelation of Christ, "upon this rock I will build my church." Friends, this is where judgment of others comes in: In order to look at someone else, you first have to stop looking at Jesus. We point fingers at our brothers when we fail to sit in the presence of Christ.

6. Martha says that Mary "has left me to do all this serving alone..." It is now clearly revealed what exactly that is: the root of loneliness, abandonment and that feeling that we ourselves and our group are the only ones actually doing anything for God. We have made up our own ministry and have let it eclipse God Himself. Always remember that Martha is bent against Mary. She doesn't understand her and feels she is unprofitable, unsuccessful, and simply unwilling to work. Martha's work mentality cannot even fathom the eternal significance of Mary's attentiveness to and stillness before the Lord, for the short-lived self-imposed task has eclipsed the presence of Jesus.

7. Martha begins to tell Jesus what to do, as if she knows better than He what is needed in the moment: "tell her

to help me..." So much "intercession" today is like this: one person looking at another person with his or her own opinion of what God should do and asking Him to change the other person. We humans are peculiar creatures when we try to correct God, like mosquitoes trying to correct a rocket scientist. Martha prays to cure her sister's "slothfulness," for the needs of the Lord must be met, and Jesus Himself must be told how it needs to be done. She prays to the Lord, "speak to my sister. Change her heart. Move in her to take seriously the service that I know is fit for the King." All this while, Christ is flowing into Mary. Mary's attention is so fixed upon Christ, she is probably not even aware of Martha and her accusations. Even if Mary can hear the reproach, she is silent to it; she offers no rebuttal for herself, just like the Lamb that she looks to. I have a feeling Mary was blind and deaf to all else going on around her. She doesn't interrupt her Lord with frustrations about Martha because she is too preoccupied with His beauty to critique her sister's flaws. I am almost positive she forgot Martha was even in the same house.

8. The Lord answers, "Martha, Martha..." The fact that the Lord says her name twice is interesting to me. There are several times when God does this in the Scriptures: The summoning of Paul ("Saul, Saul"), the choosing of Samuel ("Samuel, Samuel"), the calling of Moses ("Moses, Moses"), and the mourning over Israel ("Jerusalem, Jerusalem") to name a few. Now Jesus points to another significant issue in Martha's life by saying her name. The precious God-man, in whom the fullness of the God-head dwells in bodily form, directly addresses this performing and striving soul. God Himself describes her scattered condition.

9. Jesus exposes her doubts and fears when He says, "You are worried." Don't miss this! How do we become worn and withered from anxiety? How do apprehensions, doubts and fears enter in? Herein lies the origin of our troubled hearts: a deviated gaze. When you stop looking to Jesus, you sink. Just ask Peter.

10. Jesus unveils another layer of Martha's issue when He says she is "bothered." A disturbed and disquieted soul is the symptom of a distracted gaze. Friends, mark this down in your internal notebook: when you feel internally troubled, it indicates a preoccupation. It is time to get still in His presence and turn your eyes to Jesus and hear His voice. Internal unrest is the warning of the Holy Ghost.

11. Jesus says these three revealing words, "so many things." The multiplicity of our own ways erodes us if we do not live at His feet. Men get exhausted when they fail to exhaust the riches of Christ.[2]

ONE THING IS NECESSARY

What many people do not understand is that the soul was made to do all things while looking at Jesus so that everything done—whether eating or drinking, cleaning or working, preaching or praying, teaching or counseling — is done unto the glory of God. But God only receives glory when our works issue from a continuous state of adoration and fixation upon Him. While Martha's actions issued from what she was doing, Mary's legacy was rooted in who she was.

Jesus coins the phrase tattooed on the heart of every love-sick believer: "only one thing is necessary." Jesus frankly states that His presence and voice are the only essential things.

Martha's labors were unneeded, unnecessary and pointless, simply because they were from a different realm. Naturally they were significant, for who wouldn't serve Jesus if He came to their house, it is in a woman's nature to serve; even Peter's mother-in-law waited on Jesus as soon as He raised her up from her sick bed. But, even though the natural mind sees this service as significant, God calls us into a higher realm, specifically, to conform us to the image of His Son through the receiving of His presence and voice. He is after an experiential union that only comes through an experiential fellowship. We must realize that the realm of human service has never pleased God because only God pleases God. Witness Lee said, "even if you could submit to God on your own, it wouldn't please God because God is only pleased with His Son." The only thing that pleases God is what He does Himself. Mary is in the "becoming" realm where contemplation and activity are united in being. That is what God is after: men who *become* the message, who plunge themselves into Him and become like Him. Sons of God will say with Jesus, "I can do nothing on My own," and will live as Jesus, "My Father abiding in Me does His works."

THE CHOICE IS YOURS

Jesus says, "Mary has chosen." The tragedy about this picture is the equally available Christ and our freedom to not choose Him. Martha preferred what made sense to her, what was naturally and outwardly acceptable as service. In direct contrast, Mary chose "the good part": His presence, His face, and His voice by drawing near, bowing low and gazing attentively upon Him.₃ I tell you that the good fruit from the good tree comes from choosing the good part, which is eating from the hand of the Good Shepherd. This life is as indestructible as God, for Jesus says it "shall not be taken away from her." Because this reception of God is of true eternal significance, it cannot be lost.

CONCLUSION

Maybe this concept of being in God's presence is foreign to you. My heart breaks for those who have only known adherence to rules and restrictions, service and duty. God never had that kind of life in mind. He sent His own Son to the earth in order to bring the relationship He has with the Son to us. He endured separation from the Son to reconcile man to Himself and restore blissful union with us. Those who have received His Spirit are His very own family. There is no analogy that can sufficiently convey what His Life is like for it is in a category all by itself, but I promise that if you will lay your life down to live dependently upon His presence, you will receive a constant flow of life on the inside that works in you both to will and do for His good pleasure.[4] Art Katz once said, "Sonship is when you cannot tell where the one begins and the other ends." Jesus refused to do anything outside of spiritually perceiving God's desires. We must recognize that apart from Him we are impotent, but when we choose to do only what He is doing, He causes His own works to be ours.

---

1 John 6:63

2. Isaiah 57:10

3 I am not saying that everyone should lock themselves in their rooms and never do anything for God, scared to move outside of Him and frozen in inactivity in the name of bliss. In fact, anyone who claims to be in deep fellowship with the Spirit and does not preach the gospel and waste their life on Jesus is in a dangerous delusion probably influenced greatly by some demonic deception. I am saying that everything that we do: planning, preaching, counseling, outreach, etc....should issue spontaneously out of what we are in delightful union with Him. Those who see, speak. In many cases silent mouths are empty souls.

4 Philippians 2:13

CHAPTER TWO

DELIGHT
IN THE DIVINE

"When you stand in prayer and feel that no other joy can be compared to it, then you have indeed discovered true prayer."
-Evagrios of Pontus

"If you are tired and worn out by your labors, recline upon His breast, breathe in the fragrant Spirit of Life, and allow Life to permeate your being. Rest upon Him, for He is a table of refreshment that will serve you the food of the divine Father."
-John of Dalyutha

Speaking of the soul in prayer – "...it will be so touched with delight that it will no longer want to leave that place..."
-Symeon the New Theologian

"Above everything else, as fulfillment of the New Covenant the Spirit marked the return of the lost presence of God."
-Gordon Fee

DELIGHT IN THE DIVINE

"How lovely are Your dwelling places."
~Psalm 84:1

The devotional pen of the man after God's own heart drips with a violent Shakespearian love of God's presence. David's love relationship with God is a glorious romance as they constantly exchange the sweet experience of one another. He writes the word "lovely" which means "very pleasant, enjoyable and delightful." Do you know that the place where God rests is full of delight and pleasure because He Himself is the highest delight and pleasure? Even before the cross and Pentecost, the Scriptures are engraved with this blessed experiential promise: "In the presence of the Lord is fullness of joy and pleasure forevermore."[1]

A life in His presence is full of rapturous delight and deep internal enjoyment. The word, "enjoy" means "to take pleasure in." Make no mistake; the dwelling of God is richly experiential. He longs to fill us with the finest of wheat and satisfy us with honey from the rock, for He is the very rock from which we receive the honey.[2] Men take refuge under the shadow of His wings and drink their fill from the abundance of His house. He gives us to drink from the river of His delights. For in His presence is the fountain of life and He Himself is the fountain of living water.[3]

DELIGHT

The king writes expressively, "how lovely..." (pleasurable and delightful) "are your dwelling places." Elsewhere he writes, "I love the habitation of your house and the place where your glory dwells."[4] The dwelling place of God is so experiential that the whole of the king's being — his mind, will and emotions — long to experience Him. Like a hungry steak lover waiting in a steak house salivates at the sights and smells around him, so David anticipates experiencing God's presence. "My soul longs and even yearns for the courts of the Lord." In the King James Version of the Bible the word "pines" is used. This word means "to suffer out of desire for." Using the following verse as a commentary we see an unfolding of this blissful longing. I can almost see David's diadem tottering as he throws his head back in expression: "my heart and my flesh sing for joy..."

The joy of the Lord starts with the internal person. The world's happiness depends primarily upon external things, while God increases man's joy from his inner being. Elsewhere the Psalmist writes, "You have put joy in my heart more than the time when my corn and my wine increased."[5] When everything has gone well for us, and we have had an abundance of riches, and when the influence of wine runs through our veins bringing merriment, God brings more delight and bliss than even these pleasures.

EXPERIENCE

In our current passage, David doesn't say "my flesh and my heart" but rather "my heart and my flesh," explaining that the experience overflows into the body from the heart. The eruption of internal joy floods the outer man as well. "As one grows in prayer, these gentle beginnings slowly develop in both intensity and duration. The desires become ardent yearnings and burning thirsting for God...we are so one that inter-influence between spiritual and material is unavoidable."[6]

St. John of the Cross writes, "Sometimes the unction of the Holy Spirit overflows into the body and all the sensory substance, all the members and bones and marrow rejoice...with the feeling of great delight and glory even in the outer most joints of the hands and feet."[7] This experiential fellowship with God colors the faces of all those who have interacted with Him. "They that look to Him are radiant."[8] When you stand in the direct sunlight can you not feel the heat on your skin? If you bask in the sun light for a while, will the skin on your face not change? If the direct radiance of the sun changes your face as you bask in it, how much more will your face be changed by basking in the divine rays of the Son of God? Friends, we are seated with Christ in heavenly places and this experiential ecstasy makes that reality perceptible.

Richard Rolle writes that when we experience Jesus, He becomes "all your desire, all your joy, all your consolation, all your strength, so that your song will always be about Him, and in Him all your rest."[9] He describes a sense of God's presence in this manner: "...a certain sweet gift flows into the pure mind, and, as if drunk with strong wine, she melts into the pleasure of the Creator."[10] He prays, "Inebriate my spirit with the burning wine of your sweetest love, so that, forgetting all evils and all limited sights, illusions and images, I may exult, embracing you alone, and I may rejoice in God my Jesus."[11]

If this has not been your experience up until now in your Christian life, it does not mean that it is not supposed to be or that it cannot be. The ecstasy of life is God Himself. His presence and His rule should be the source of all our joy and peace, for His rule is in His presence and His presence is in His rule. Angela of Foligno speaks of "extreme delight that I feel I want to always remain in this state."[12] She writes, "My soul then felt that God was in me and I knew this to be true because of the spiritual joy and holy delight which I experienced..." And another, "All the members of my body thrilled with delights as I lay in this experience."

David's language is no different: "How blessed is the man who dwells in Your house." He equates blessing in life with a life dwelling in God's presence. If there is any kind of endorsement of a blessed life in Christianity, let it be this life lived in the sweet presence of Jesus. Let it be, that our outward circumstances in life have no bearing on whether or not we have joy and peace, simply because our joy and peace are found in the Person and presence of Jesus. David writes, "They are ever praising You." Those who live in the presence of Jesus live in a constant state of praise, and when they gather together, they erupt in praise. The presence of Jesus assembles all who follow Christ into His house, inviting us to dwell there. I submit to you that a major part of the disunity in the church indicates a lack of the dwelling in the house of the Lord. We have erected our own houses instead of moving into His house and His presence. He will not permit a dual lodging; we must make our home in Him and He will make His home in us.

PRODUCT OF PRESENCE

Notice a listed effect of the life that chooses to make its dwelling in the presence of God: "Blessed is the man whose strength is in You." The phrases are used one after another as an expounding upon one another. They are even interchangeable. Blessing is in dwelling in God and drawing your strength from God is dwelling in God. The one who doesn't make God his dwelling doesn't make God his strength. The one who fails to make God his source of strength fails to dwell in God's presence. To seek strength apart from God's empowering presence is to indirectly believe that the power of human resolve is greater. We cannot lean upon the arm or strength of the flesh; His presence is strength and strength is His presence.

INTERNAL ROUTE

How do we get to the house of the Lord? "...in whose heart is the highways to Zion." The route to the place of God is in the heart of man. He no longer dwells in temples made by the hands of men but settles in the hearts of men. God makes His residence in you because you make your residence in Him. The only way to enter His house is to invite His internal residence in your heart. In the Amplified Version of the Bible 1 John 3:24 says,

"All who keep His commandments [who obey His orders and follow His plan, live and continue to live, to stay and] abide in Him, and He in them. [They let Christ be a home to them and they are the home of Christ.] And by this we know and understand and have the proof that He [really] lives and makes His home in us: by the [Holy] Spirit Whom He has given us."

The evidence that He dwells with us is found in the presence of His Spirit. We are protected by this indwelling presence as the Amplified also states in 1 John 5:

"We know [absolutely] that anyone born of God does not [deliberately and knowingly] practice committing sin, but the One Who was begotten of God carefully watches over and protects him [Christ's divine presence within him preserves him against the evil], and the wicked one does not lay hold (get a grip) on him or touch [him]." The presence of the Spirit is an undeniable living reality that cannot be separated from the experience of His

person. The daily walk with God is no less experiential than our initial encounter with Him. David points to this reality.

DWELLING IN HIS PRESENCE

In verse six, David states that the one who dwells in the presence of God — not just positional but experiential — will, "pass through the valley of sorrow (Baca) and make it a Spring." Cure D'Ars said, "In the soul united with God it is always springtime." Is such a view of God's presence too good to be true? Many times I have been accused of presenting God encounters as "sunshine and rainbows." I don't understand this, because in all of His characteristics, He is the bliss of life. Even when sin sets the world on fire, God is still wonderful. Even when He makes judgment on the world, the children of His kingdom will see His glory. His obedient followers constantly live under the Shadow of His wings. Christians who have gone through times of persecution and torture give amazing accounts of Christ's blissful presence. Heaven is always heaven, God is always God, and the presence is always the presence. Even in the most difficult times of life, He is a refuge for us. This really makes us different. His presence is our distinguishing factor; in the Old Testament the Children of Israel where just another people-group without His presence. When the world around us crumbles, and we have nothing left, He still sets His bow in the sky to remind us that, "The future is as bright as the promises of God."[13] For the one who makes the house of the Lord his dwelling place, "the early rain covers [his life] with blessing". The valley of sorrow becomes a spring, and the early rain falls on it causing fruitfulness and life.

INCREASE IN HIS PRESENCE

"They go from strength to strength." Increase is the result of the presence of God; the lovely dwelling place of God brings us from one degree of strength to the next. How is it that so many Christians stay spiritually feeble all their lives? How do they remain spiritual babes for 20 years straight? How is it possible they remain at one level and never mature? It is because they do not constantly reside in the lovely dwelling place of God. Friend, do you live in His house and experience the ecstasies of His delightful face? Does His presence flood your heart with joy every day? Is His presence the source of your peace in the midst of daily chaos, or do fear and external circumstances overwhelm you? If we Christians have any distinguishing factor from the world it should be that we live under and find our joy, delight and peace in the Shadow of the Almighty. If we don't have fellowship with Him, how can we claim union with Him?

"For a day in Your courts is better than a thousand elsewhere. I would rather stand at the threshold of the house of my God than dwell in the tents of wickedness." Do you feel the urging of this man after God's own heart? In essence, he is saying, "One day with God, one 24 hour period in His presence is more valuable, more delightful, and more fulfilling than millions of hours doing anything else or being anywhere else in the world. Even if I couldn't enter into His house, it is far better to stand at the threshold and smell the fragrance of that place than to live a life in the greatest pleasures of the world." Sex, drugs, food, fame, riches, or anything you can think of, pales in comparison to the experiential bliss of being near Jesus in His radiant glory.

YOU WERE MADE FOR HIS PRESENCE

The Lord's presence is the greatest delight of my existence, not because I have trained myself in religious discipline, but because my soul is captivated by the spiritual sight, sound, and touch of God. People say to me all the time, "You have to learn to acquire a taste for God," like He is an avocado or a hobby. No, there is nothing as tasty or pleasurable as the Lord. If your experience of God is something you must acquire a taste for, it is not God. I have seen drug addicts and sex addicts receive one touch from God and never return to those lesser pleasures again. I have seen grown men hardened by life and sin fall on their faces and weep like little girls as God manifested His presence to them. Yes, they were convicted of their sin, but that is only part of it; they encountered the glory of God as the missing piece of their existence and fell head over heels in love with Jesus Christ from just one glimpse of His face.

GIFT OF GLORY

The glory of God in the face of Jesus Christ is a gift to those who choose Him. "For the Lord is a sun and shield He gives grace and glory." What a gift! The illumination of His presence causes us to see and gives us His grace and glory. "How blessed are those who dwell in Your house. How blessed is the man whose strength is in You... How blessed is the man who trusts in You." The life that dwells in the house of God finds its strength in Him and anchors its trust in Him. Dwelling, drawing and trusting: We dwell in Him, we trust in Him and we draw strength from Him. Let me conclude this chapter with a short quote from Witness Lee:

In Matthew chapter one, we are told that Christ was called Emmanuel, which means "God with us." I really like those two words, "with us." This does not mean that we have a specific doctrine or know the teaching, nor does it mean that we keep a kind of ritual or have any forms. It means that we have His very presence with us. His being with us is everything. What does it mean to be religious? To be religious means to have all the scriptural things, all the fundamental things, and yet lack the presence of the Lord. How wonderful it is to have the presence of the Bridegroom with us. Do you need comfort? His presence is your comfort. Do you need life? His presence is your life. Do you need anything else? I tell you, His presence is everything to you. If you have His presence you have everything. Oh the Bridegroom is with us.[14]

---

1 Psalm 16:11

2 Psalm 81:16;Duet 32:13

3 See Psalm 36 and Jeremiah chapter 2

4 Psalm 26:8

5 Psalm 4:7

6 Thomas Dubay, S.M., *Fire Within* (San Francisco: Ignatius Press, 1989) p. 42, 43.

7 Thomas Dubay, S.M. *Fire Within* (San Francisco: Ignatius Press, 1989) p. 43.

8 Psalm 34:5

9 Richard Rolle, *The English Writings* (New York: Paulist Press, 1988) p. 32.

10 Richard Rolle, *The English Writings* (New York: Paulist Press, 1988) p. 28

11 Richard Rolle, *The English Writings* (New York: Paulist Press, 1988) p. 29

12 Angela of Foligno, *Complete Works* (New York: Paulist Press, 1993) p.158, 157, 148

13 Adoniram Judson

14 Witness Lee, *Christ versus Religion* (Anaheim, CA; Living Stream Ministry, 1971) p. 17.

Into The Cloud

CHAPTER THREE

THE
REVELATION
OF JESUS

Jesus is the target of all the arrows of religion."
-Witness Lee

"The most attractive and spiritual things in Christianity – if they are outside of Christ – are but dead. We should let the Lord himself be this thing or that to us. Then it is living. It is living both in us and in those who receive us."
-Watchman Nee

"If Christ is not life then we need to do the work. But if Christ is life then we need not struggle."
-Watchman Nee

"...the Father of glory, may give to you a spirit of wisdom and revelation in the recognition of Him..."
-St. Paul, Ephesians 1:17 Young's Literal Translation

THE REVELATION OF JESUS

"When they lifted their eyes they saw no man, but Jesus only." ~Matthew 17:8 NASB

Why are Christians today so concerned with trivial things? As we learned in chapter 1, I believe that many, like Martha, have taken their eyes off of Christ. Why is it so rare to find a person who is set and fixed on Jesus alone? One falls off to the left, another falls off to the right, and yet Jesus remains the same.[1] Instead of looking at wayward messages and pointing out the inaccuracies in teachers and preachers today, let us search the text of Matthew 17:1-8 to find an incredible spiritual itinerary of how to live a life fixed upon Jesus.[2]

1. SEPARATION

"Jesus took with Him Peter and James and John his brother, and led them up on a high mountain by themselves."

First, Christ separated these specific individuals from the rest. The first secret to a life focused upon Jesus is seasons of separation from the world and others to be alone with Him. It is imperative to get away with Him. Why is this so important if we live in perpetual fellowship with Him throughout the day? The simple answer is because the secret place is the power of the abiding place; the foundation of your life in Him in public is receiving life from Him in private. I don't mean to make any one uncomfortable, but the truth is that just as there are certain things a husband and wife will do only when they're alone together, there are certain things Jesus will only do with you when you are alone with Him.

When Jesus taught on prayer in the sixth chapter of Matthew He said, "...go into your closet..." This is separation. Leave the company of others and get alone. Then He said, "...shut the door..." He not only wants us to separate ourselves, but He also wants us to shut out the noise. Separation, solitude and silence are the siblings of prayer. As Art Katz, a mighty spokesman of God, once said, you must "...be ruthless with yourself to get alone, lock the door and seek God and be found by Him."

In John 3:22 the Scripture says, *"After these things Jesus and His disciples went into the land of Judea and there He was spending time with them..."*

Here are three elements of Christ's discipleship:

1. Without time there can be no discipleship. The number one seed sown into your life to yield forth an increase is time. Time is our spiritual fermentation.

2. What kind of time? It is time *with Him*, being in the presence of Jesus, which will miraculously fashion us into true followers of Jesus. Andrew Murray said, "Christ's presence was the training of the disciples."

3. When you "spend time with someone," it is not a matter of simply sitting with them, but rather communicating and exchanging with that individual. When we spend time with Jesus, His voice and presence disciples and guide us.

Thomas Merton wrote, "Without solitude of some sort, there is and can be no maturity." He continues: "There must be a time of day when the man who makes plans forgets his plans, and acts as if he had no plans at all. There must be a time of day when the man who has to speak falls very silent. And his mind forms no more propositions...There must be a time when the man of resolutions puts aside his resolutions as if they had all been broken..."₃

2. LEADING

Here is the second point: He "led them..." We must be led by God. We cannot get alone for the mere sake of solitude; we must separate ourselves in His particular way, totally submitted to His divine will and following His every step. Dr. Robert Gladstone spoke of "walking in rhythm with God." This wonderful picture immediately reminds me of 2 John: "I have no greater joy than to see my children walking in the truth." Step by step, moment by moment; what we will be in our final moment is the sum total of what we were in all our moments. It is only in subjection to Him that we will ascend the mountain of prayer. The defiant cannot pray simply because they are self-sufficient. As Leonard Ravenhill said, "you can't have pride and pray. Prayer is the practice of the poor." The heights of this kind of prayer are not for the ones who have only claimed Him, but for those who will go with Him, who will leave the others behind and follow the momentary movements of Christ.

Have you experienced the tender pulling of the Spirit? Charles Finney wrote, "Cherish the slightest impressions of the Spirit." The other disciples did follow Jesus, but they were not party to certain moments that Peter, James, and John experienced, including this ascension up the mountain. The mountain represents the ecstatic heights of ascended prayer and communion, when one is above the earth and in the presence of God.₄ This suspended life knows no more union with the earth, as is evidenced in the life of Christ while He Himself was suspended on the cross, breaking gravity in the ascension to heaven, and sending the Holy Spirit to those praying and waiting in the upper room. These who followed the momentary movements of the Son ascended into prayer that transcends information and produces transformation.

3. REVELATION

"He was transfigured before them; and His face shone like the sun, and His garments became as white as light."

After bringing the disciples high upon the mountain with Him, Jesus unveiled Himself to them. Dear reader, Jesus has something He wants to show you. Do you know what it is? It is a revelation of Himself. He wants to raise your life above the earth and transform it with the radiance of his person. All who followed Jesus had a revelation of Him, but those who followed Him up into the mountain of communion had a greater revelation of Him. Few people get alone with God but even fewer follow the leading of Christ where they receive that "great unveiling."

Christ always leads us into a revelation of Himself, for God has nothing more precious to offer us than His own person. Here, in detail, is the desire of Christ: to separate you from everyone else and lead you into a greater vision of Himself. This unveiling, this revelation, this illumination, is Christ. "The way which God gives is Christ, the truth which God gives is also Christ and the life which God gives is likewise Christ. Christ is our way, Christ is our truth, Christ is our life. It is through Christ that we come to the Father...What He gives to us is Christ Himself."

4. THE VOICE OF THE FATHER

"…a bright cloud overshadowed them, and behold, a voice out of the cloud said, 'This is My beloved Son, with whom I am well-pleased; listen to Him!'"

When Jesus revealed Himself to His disciples, they heard God the Father's voice. In the presence of the Son, we hear the Father and through the speaking of the Father we see the Son. The Father confirms the Son and says "listen to Him." This doesn't just mean "do what He says," but also means: GIVE ALL YOUR ATTENTION TO THE SON. We must be sure to not miss what He will say. Here lies the major issue: we have given our attention to other things. Perhaps, we have looked intently at the brightness of His clothes, the light from His face, the hovering glory, or even Moses and Elijah. But God, while not condemning or diminishing the bi-products of His manifest glory, pinpoints the prime element of the glory of God — Jesus Himself. Though all these manifestations are from Christ and cannot be found apart from Him, He Himself must be our focus.

In response to the Son's breathtaking unveiling and the Father's thunderous speaking, the disciples fall on their faces. Is there a better picture of humility and worship in the human life than falling on our faces before God? Humility is the only right response to seeing the glory and hearing the voice of God, for its origin was, is, and always will be, in a vision of Jesus. When men see Him, they become nothing — Jesus takes the stage and all others fade away. It was Andrew Murray who wrote, "…we are never more humble than when we adore Him."

5. DIRECT CONTACT

At this point one might ask, "What else is there? Could there really be more than that?" I submit this next point to you as a bi-product of the last. "He came to them." It is crucial to understand that Jesus responds to the disciple's humility by drawing even nearer. Not only do they see the glory of the Son and hear the voice of the Father, but as they cast themselves to the earth in humble adoration, are approached by the Son. Jesus touches them. Direct contact through the revelation of the Son in the presence of God is the most transformative work there is. Jacob's whole walk was changed after a touch on the hip; the dead boy being carried out of the city in a coffin was raised by one touch of His hand; multitudes were healed by simply receiving His touch. The hand of Christ is the channel through which the electric current of God's very person flows. For these disciples, the specific result of having been touched by Him was this: "When they lifted up their eyes they saw nothing else but Jesus alone." The secret to a sustained vision of Jesus is direct contact with God, and the secret to direct contact with God is a sustained vision of Jesus.

It is interesting to note that the three men who shared this encounter were three distinctly different individuals whose callings were vastly different. I believe they point to three specific kinds of believers that an exchange with Christ produces. First, James was one of the earliest martyrs of the church, representing the Spirit of martyrdom. Direct contact with God will produce people who are willing to lay their heads upon the block for Christ, fearless before the spirit of the world. Second, Peter's shadow healed the sick; I believe he represents carrying the glory of God. Direct contact with Christ will produce carriers of God's glory. As Bill Johnson said, "Your shadow will release whatever overshadows you." Lastly, John is the beloved disciple. Direct contact with God will produce love-sick revelators who can access the divine Person and rest their heads upon His breast.

This kind of bridal union and contact with Jesus is articulated so well by Mother Basilea Schlink:

"I come to live within you."
Our Lord and Savior Jesus says this to every Christian soul.
Prepare for me a lodging with ardent love and longing, that I may with your soul unite.
Prepare your hearts chamber, put far all earthly Clamor, silence all worldly longings now.
Upon you take my quietness, eternities own stillness, and my approaching footsteps here.
Give up your will entirely, surrender all completely to me, and to my will be given. Then can I make my dwelling, within your heart now reigning, one then with you and love and pain.
What then could be more glorious or sweeter than your presence within my heart, oh Jesus Christ? Now all with any silence that you may come to enter myself and make it yours. [5]

"He will live only in hearts that love Him. Only there does He desire to dwell. Loving Him means giving Him first place. It means nothing can stir our hearts as He does. We need to be on our guard against being overwhelmed by earth's joys and sorrows, by our work and activities.

When such things preoccupy us, Jesus no longer has first place in our lives and has to leave the innermost chamber of our heart. Nothing that concerns, excites, or upsets us should be allowed to penetrate into that sanctuary where He lives and has His throne. Ultimately, nothing should disquiet us because He who is our peace is living in the deepest recesses of our heart. For bridal souls, there is no greater fear then losing their first love by being absorbed with the joys and troubles and the ups and downs of daily life. He requires of us total devotion: He will not share the throne of our hearts with anyone or anything else. He will not have us dominated by troubles, cares, people, or the things of this world. This is why a bridal soul wholeheartedly resists all such influences that might take control of her. He alone is to reign in her. His indwelling is her greatest joy and happiness. All this means she has a deep inner peace regardless of any external pressures and troubles weighing upon her. She is always one with him, he and her and she and him."[6]

---

1 Hebrews 13:8

2 A "spiritual itinerary" is a term used to speak of the stages of progression into union with God.

3 Thomas Merton, An Invitation to the Contemplative Life (The Word Among Us Press: Ijamsville, Maryland, 2006), p. 92.

4 Luke 6:12; 9:28; John 4:20;Mark 6:46

5 Basilea Schlink, *My All For Him* (Minnesota: Bethany House Publishers, 1999) p. 81.

6 Basilea Schlink, My All For Him (Bloomington, Minnesota: Bethany House publishers, 1999) p. 81-83.

CHAPTER FOUR

REASON VS REVELATION

"Reason is sight by a created light. Revelation is sight by the Uncreated Light."
-John Ruusbroec

"For it is not mere words that nourish the soul, but God Himself, and unless and until the hearers find God in personal experience, they are not the better for having heard the truth. The Bible is not an end in itself, but a means to bring men to an intimate and satisfying knowledge of God, that they may enter into Him, that they may delight in His Presence, may taste and know the inner sweetness of the very God Himself in the core and center of their hearts."
-A.W.Tozer

REASON VS REVELATION

"They plotted together to seize Jesus by stealth and kill Him."

~Matthew 26:3

I wish to draw from Matthew 26:1-13 some very important points concerning how the spirits of religion and reason wage war against the Spirit of revelation. Beneath the plaintext we can unveil their plans to steal, kill, and destroy the revelation of Christ and the joy that He wants to offer us.

RELIGION

In the first five verses we see the Pharisees secretly plotting against Jesus' life. The text is simple: they sought to kill the Word made flesh. By the revelation of the Holy Spirit we can understand a deeper revelation: the word of Life is hated and attacked by the spirit of religion. Jesus is the very way, truth and Life of God, and that which is false will always despise that which is true. Not only has this opposition been seen in the life of Christ, but also in the lives of the prophets and apostles, those who carried His word; concerning the Spirit of life versus the spirit of religion, it will always be this way. Until the Son of man returns, the powers of the air will influence men against the Life of God and the reason of men will be offended with the wisdom of God.

Friend, keep this ever and always at the forefront of your mind: because of its authenticity, the revelation of Christ is hated by religion and reason. The life of God is hated by religion, and whenever the Life of God is present, the religious spirit will plot against Him with the intent to put a stop to His work; religion's sole purpose is to snuff out the Life of God.

He will let you have every element; his only concern is that you're not connected to the power source. You can have multiple appliances at your house, but they are useless without power. As Leonard Ravenhill said, "You may have the nicest car, the cleanest car, and the fastest car, but if there is no spark in the engine you are finished." The spirit of religion is only nervous when the life of God is present: you can hold conferences, memorize scriptures, pray for hours, and witness daily but when you operate without the presence of the Holy Spirit, he yawns at your life.

The religious spirit operating in the cold hearts of the Pharisees caused their frozen hearts to value religion, tradition, ordinances and self-devotion without the life of God. At every point, the spirit of religion is empty, dark, void and powerless, resisting the vibrant, living, growing and powerful Word at every point.

RELIGION'S MIND

The religious leaders operating under lifeless traditions and ordinances and ignoring the life of God in their own selfishness contested Jesus, the Word of life, at every point. Times have not changed: if you are filled with the Word of Life, Religion will fight you as well. Before he went on to be with the Lord, Art Katz once said concerning the life of God: "Paul was so ostensible the visible statement of the life of Christ that the conclusion over his life was that this man is not fit to live."

The Scripture gives us another detail about the spirit of religion: "they were afraid of the people." The religious spirit is always people conscious, explaining why the Pharisees wanted to seize Jesus in stealth, which means quietly and secretly. This is exactly the way that the spirit of religion works; it is extremely conscious of what other people think, so it must manipulate and scheme so as to not be too obvious.

It is also very interesting to note that the leaders sought to seize Jesus *before* killing Him. Seizing him is symbolic of taking him under their control; therefore the religious spirit operates under a need for control. It doesn't initially kill, but rather seeks first to seize; under multiple guises, it manipulates until it has you under its control, saying things like, "He is a danger, he is rebellious, he is..." Whether or not it is perceived in the beginning, the desired end is to steal, kill and destroy the influence of the Life of God.

REASON

Tony Kemp, an incredible man of faith and the Spirit, says, "Where reason is prevalent revelation is missing." Reason cannot come unto Jesus "for the light of faith demands that a man transcend the scope of his own reason." Even if reason enters His presence it has nothing to offer him. Reason is provoked by revelation because it can't find value in revelation. Where revelation produces worship, reason produces judgment. Reason and worship never mix because reason can only see humanism and elevates the self over adoration of Jesus. Reason doesn't value Christ's presence and Christ exposes reason's ill motives. Revelation trumps reason because reason is so far inferior to the revelation of Christ. Where reason is sight by a created light, revelation is sight by the uncreated light.

JESUS' RESPONSE

So how did Jesus handle the religious ones? To those who were open, he preached the life that embodied, seeking to give Himself to them and calling them to enter into Him. To those who closed themselves off, He exposed their hypocrisy, declaring that they knew what God *had said* yet didn't care about what God *was saying* while claiming to be in obedience to Him; they were so blinded by the letter of the law that they were unable to hear God. The religious spirit "devotes" itself to God without receiving the life of God. You can be assured that where the life of God is absent, religion is present; it lacks the word of life, only providing evidence of death. As previously stated, religion knows only what God has said and nothing of what God is saying.

WINE OF HEAVEN

Friends, religion cannot exist in the one who drinks and eats of Him! The antidote to the lethargy and stench of death from the spirit of religion is the bread of life and the river of the Lord's delights. Jesus gives us wine to drink! Wine represents joy, feasting, laughter, and intoxication; His presence frees us from the need to have anything other than Him. Maybe you should read that last statement again: His presence frees us from the need to have anything other than Him!

Wine is compared to the filling of the Spirit in Ephesians 5:18. Have you been so intoxicated by the presence of the Spirit that you may have appeared drunk to an outsider? In Acts 2, when the Holy Spirit is poured out on the apostles, outsiders thought that they were drunk. Peter says, "These men are not drunk...as you suppose..." They were drunk, but not with natural wine. The influence of the Holy Spirit had come upon them and intoxicated them away from all self-consciousness.

Wine bursts the religious system in Luke 5:33-39. Does this even need to be expounded upon? The religious devil and his program are never emptier to us than when we are filled with the Spirit.

Wine is the element used to heal the wounded in Luke 10:34. So many people have been mistreated, burned and beaten by this world and the religious spirit operating in it. The two elements used to heal the wounds inflicted by the world system are none other than "oil and wine." How wonderful! God heals us by dispensing Himself into us. We do not just need a new mindset; therapy and psychiatric sessions alone will not heal our souls; we desperately need to drink...of the Holy Spirit. You can bathe in wine, but it will not affect your body until you imbibe it. Theology will never perform what the wine of the Spirit can.

Wine symbolizes the blood, which is life, specifically HIS LIFE. That is why the wine is the drink of the New Covenant and His blood is the life of the New Covenant. In Matthew 26, after offering the Bread of Life to His disciples, Jesus also offers a cup of wine. It is a gift from the Lord, this Wine of Life, this Spiritual draft and intoxicating drink from the hand of Christ. Will you reject this cup? Many are afraid of what might happen to them, but I promise that the reception of the Spirit of Jesus Christ will only cause you to be more like Him.

Wine is symbolic of the experience of love in Song of Solomon 1:2. His love is not just a theory or a concept. He gives and pours His own blood into us through the Cross. Because Thou didst thirst upon the tree, Thou are new wine to me.

Wisdom has given us wine to drink in Proverbs 9:5. Lady Wisdom's great revelations are united with experiencing the wine of heaven: she releases such a glass of revelation that if one drinks it they will be filled with the Spirit. Proverbs 1:26 shows us that if we repent and receive reproof, God will pour His Spirit upon us and make His words known to us. He gives revelation in connection with wine and wine releases revelation.

Psalm 104:15 says, "...wine which makes the heart glad, so that he may make his face glistening with oil." That which we put into us will inevitably flow out of us; if we choose His wine, His oil will glisten from our faces. Many times, the faces of the beloved ones have glowed with the radiant presence of God; I promise you that this glistening only comes from receiving the wine that makes the heart glad. Friends, Jesus gives us wine to drink. Of all the things that Jesus could have done to prepare the disciples to preach the gospel, He chose to pour wine out from heaven.

JOY

Wine breeds joy and joy transcends all reason. One indication of the religious spirit is that there is no joy. Because religion doesn't have joy, it cannot give joy. The religious man does not have life in the presence of Jesus, and it is only in the presence of Jesus that we can have communion with Him, the kind of communion in which He gives Himself to us as the Bread of Life and offers us the Spirit as the cup of wine. The evidence of the King's presence is joy, for the King's domain is not a matter of what you say but rather how you live. His presence and rule is not a matter of speeches and teaching but rather a way of righteousness filled with peace and joy in the Holy Ghost.

Joy is in taking refuge in God. Psalm 5:1
Joy is in His presence. Psalm 16:11
Joy is resting in His victory. Psalm 20:5
Joy is connected to righteous living. Psalm 30:11
God is Joy. Psalm 33:1
Joy is in His rule. Psalm 43:14

Joy is in hearing Him. Psalm 48:2
Joy is in repentance. Psalm 51:8,12
Joy is in His shadow. Psalm 63:7
Joy is in His presence. Psalm 84:2
Joy is the springs of God. Psalm 87:7
Joy is our satisfaction. Psalm 90:14
Joy is in the presence of God, Psalm 95:2
Joy is shed abroad in our hearts, by the Holy Spirit. Romans 15:30
Joy is our way of life. 1 Thessalonians 5:16
Joy is our strength. Nehemiah 8
Joy is the fruit of the first fruits of the Spirit. Galatians 5:22

CONCLUSION

Reason and religion are hollow, false, full of death, and unable to produce fruit; they seek to manipulate, control and ultimately dam up the flow of the river of life, preventing any kind of genuine experience of God. If you are oppressed by these evil spirits and have no joy in your life, receive from the Word of Life, who is Christ, for He dispenses from Himself the wine of joy and revelation!

Into The Cloud

CHAPTER FIVE

UNION WITH GOD

"It is impossible for the preacher to keep his spirit in harmony with the divine nature...without much and constant prayer."
-E.M. Bounds

"Talking to men for God is a great thing, but talking to God for men is still greater."
-E.M. Bounds

"Apostasy begins in the closet. No man ever backslid from the life and power of Christianity who continued constant and fervent in private prayer."
-Adam Clarke

"Of all things guard against neglecting God in the prayer closet. There is nothing more fatal...how much better might I serve if I cultivate a closer communion with God."
-William Wilberforce *(written to his son)*

UNION WITH GOD

"Shall I hide from Abraham what I am about to do?"
~Psalm 99:7

It is an undeniable fact that God favored Abraham, for from the loins of Abraham's faith, God set aside a people for Himself. The chosen people of God go back to this one man's personal relationship with God. Known as the "father of faith" and the "friend of God," Abraham shares a unique and historic relationship with God. Today many love that label, "friend of God," and I know that through faith in the perfect work of the cross and the gift of the Spirit, we are all made God's very own family. But there is something that we cannot overlook about this special relationship that God shared with Abraham. I believe in the eighteenth chapter of Genesis, the Lord has revealed a progressive picture of Abraham's intimacy with God that we can tap into. Through the Spirit, I wish to unfold some amazing truths about sinking deep into the ocean of knowing God and being united with His purpose and heart.

FRIEND OF GOD

God identified Himself as the God of Abraham. Though Abraham was not perfect, God's deep relationship with him reveals the fact that He chooses to identify Himself with flawed people, simply because they believe, love, and obey Him. It is evident that Abraham's fellowship with God brought him to an incredibly intimate bond with God — he is the only man singled out in his day. This mutually affectionate relationship was a bond of covenant friends. Think of how deep this bond went, where God questioned whether or not He should keep a secret from Abraham. Did you catch that?

God actually thought to Himself, "Should I hide what I am about to do from Abraham?" God didn't share with Abraham what was coming just because He could, but because He desired to.

God's communion with Abraham was at such an intimate place that God unfolded His own future plans in no uncertain terms; Abraham was told exactly what God was going to do: where, when, why, how. And here is the most amazing part — this information was actually an invitation to intercede, an opportunity to co-labor with God. Many of us love to think that our own relationship with God is at this level of intimacy, but so few of us have actually ever been divinely shown specific future events and invited to pray through them. Do you know God like this? Is this intimacy a reality in your life? Does God desire to open His blueprints before your eyes, giving you specific details to carry out? I am not just referring to unveiling the mysteries revealed in the Scriptures concerning His plan for the ages, but also His present work in your own family, friends, church, city, and nation. This, my friend, is the definition of a covenant friend of God: someone who has God's trust. Trusting in the Lord begins this relationship; your trust in God should lead you into faithfulness to God where He can trust you.

TRUSTED BY GOD

Jesus said to the disciples, "I call you friends." These are those whom He knew had already left everything to follow Him and would eventually give their lives in faithfulness to Him. Just like Abraham, they were those with whom the Lord found it desirable and necessary to share His specifics. Can you imagine God saying to Himself, "Shall I hide from *[Insert your name]* what I am going to do?"

For example, perhaps a family member of yours has rebelled against God and is partying with other non-believers, and while you commune with God, He shares with you that the whole party is going to go up in smoke. When you recognize that information as an invitation to intercede, you begin to pray mercy and salvation for your loved one. Later you find out that a disaster did occur at the party, but a good Christian friend who felt uneasy about being there took your sister or brother away just before the catastrophe. God does many things in the earth this way, inviting us to take part in bringing the Kingdom of Heaven to earth. This is why He cherishes His friends: simply because they listen to Him, because they commune with Him, and because He can trust them. Doesn't this kind of relationship sound desirable to you?

Maybe you already live in this place. Praise God! But, I submit to you that there is always more in His heart for those who are willing to plunge into it. If you haven't experienced this, do you want to? If you have, do you want more? How do we reach this place of friendship and trust?

THE ABRAMIC ITINERARY

Notice Abraham's disposition when the Lord appears to him: "while he was sitting..." Abraham is not running, standing, leaning or even sleeping. Abraham is sitting, consciously resting, yet still and alone. Don't let this slip by unnoted: Abraham is still and at rest.

Where is he sitting? "...at the tent door." What is the significance of a tent? Well do you recall that Abraham had been called out from his home to enter a land that he did not know? He had torn his heart from his homeland and family to obey the voice of God. His life is the testimony and model of our earthly sojourning as aliens and strangers in this earth.[1]

The tent is a statement, declaring that this world was not his home and that, despite an earthly promised land, he waited for something from heaven.₂ Abraham refused to sink his feet into the soil of this earth simply because of the word that the Lord had spoken to him.

REST

Under this tent, Abraham is resting in the shade from, "the heat of the day." What a wonderful picture: Abraham rests under the shadow. Doesn't that same picture find its home in the lover of Song of Songs 2:3 ("...under His shade I took great delight and sat down...") or the Psalmist in Psalm 63:7 ("...in the shadow...I sing for joy...")? Abraham is resting, quiet, and delighting in the shade of the Most High. Friends, this is where the encounter realm is found — resting in His sweetness and hiding beneath His great love that obstructs the inevitable heat of life. Before we can understand why Abraham's friendship with God brought him into contact with the heart of God, we must understand the spiritual life that Abraham lived with God: he rested under the shadow of the Almighty; he dwelt in this place of shade; he stayed in the refuge of God. The ground for life defining encounters with God's glory is the daily experience of His glorious shadow.

WORSHIP

In the midst of the heat of life, under the shadow at the door of his tent, Abraham "lifted up his eyes." The lifting of the eyes to the Lord is a picture of worship because we choose to fix our attention above the earthly cares of life and ascend to God, moving beyond the horizontal plane into the vertical. Abraham is able to look unto God without hesitation and reservation because he has already left everything for Him. This faithful old man, having already proved God's faithfulness, neither strives nor strains but simply looks up from his place of rest in the shade. Here, in adoration, he sees. Friends, this is also where you will see; as you adore Jesus you will see Him. Abraham lifted his eyes above the world unto God and looked with his eyes, giving his attention to God's presence. And he sees three persons. Though two of these were actually angels, it is interesting to note that there appeared to him three. How utterly perfect this symbolism is: the vision is a triune vision. The vision of God is always threefold, revealing the Father by the Son, and the Son through the Spirit.

HUMILITY

It is wonderful to note that these three persons stand opposite Abraham. The vision of God is always completely opposite to what we are. Every time that we truly see Him we should be utterly convicted of how much we are not like Him, for He is holy and all together separate from all things. He is other than us at every point and our vision of Him will always reveal the same. Abraham has a vision of three persons opposite to where he is, and his vision of them infuses him with a great need to run to them. Gripped with desire, Abraham must respond. For us, all God has to do is reveal Himself and the magnetic attraction of His nature and person causes us to leave everything else behind. (I can hear the Lover sing, "Draw me and I will run after You"). Running to Him is a lover's action.

Notice that Abraham doesn't run up to the visitors and start shaking their hands as if he is like them, but he throws himself to the ground in worship. Worship always produces worship. Adoration always plunges you deeper into adoration. Abraham is humbled in adoration, low at the feet of these three.

I asked my friend Andrew Lamb₃, "If Jesus was to show up in your room one morning in prayer, what would you say to Him?" His response was amazing: "Don't leave!" Abraham says something similar: "Lord, if I have found favor in Your sight, please do not pass Your servant by." God has come to visit him and Abraham begs Him to stay.

Notice that Abraham addresses God as Lord; the kind of individual who has rich communion experiences with God is the one who submits to God as Lord. In Luke 6:46 Jesus says, "Why do you call me Lord and do not do what I command you." Today, many profess God as their Lord because they know that that is what He is supposed to be, but they refuse to submit to Him. Abraham is not this way. He acknowledges God as His Lord because he has already left everything in response to hearing God's voice.

Abraham Also calls himself the Lord's servant. A servant is someone who lives to meet the needs of another. Abraham lives to meet God's needs; he has left all. He lifts up his eyes, he looks to see God, he lays before the Lord, and he immediately longs to serve Him and seeks to be God's resting place: "Please let me wash your Feet...please rest Yourselves under the tree." I wonder if this wasn't what Jesus referenced when He said that the Father, the Son and the Spirit would make their abode in us.₄

COMMUNION

After they eat together, God speaks first to Abraham about Abraham. He looks into Abraham's heart and reminds him of the deep purpose that had been directly placed in Him, the promise He Himself had given.₅ And though God's word to him would still be tested, God speaks encouragement and

affirmation deep into Abraham's being.₆ In communion, the
first thing that God addresses is our own hearts.

SHALL I HIDE FROM ABRAHAM

After dealing with Abraham's deepest, most vulnerable parts,
God makes this statement: "Shall I hide from Abraham what I
am about to do?" Except for Christ's prayer in John 17 or
Moses' intercession for the Israelites, this statement sets in
motion perhaps the most incredible conversation recorded in
the Bible that God has with a human on behalf of humanity.
(It is important to note that both Christ and Moses deeply
encountered God before their intercessions as well.) I have
said it before and I will say it again: intercession is by
invitation only. Man does not just come up with his own plan
of Salvation and then manipulate God into it by kicking and
screaming. Intercession is a product of laying your head upon
His breast; it is hearing the vibration of God's beating heart.

Dear reader, God has called you to this very same place. He
longs to be desired and seeks to be sought. Do you live in a
tent as a sojourner and stranger in the earth, or have you sunk
your feet so deeply into the soil of this earth that you cannot
move when He calls you? Only from the stranger's tent can
one truly rest in the shade from the heat of the surrounding
desert. Even if you live detached from this filthy age, are you
resting in the shade, or are you moving and striving to make
things happen? Only from a place of rest can a man lift his
eyes and look up to God. As we wait upon Him, and focus
our attention toward Him in adoration, He will manifest
Himself and reveal the tri-unity of the Godhead. And just like
Abraham, you will know His holiness and run to Him that
you might cast yourself at His feet, looking to serve and
worship your Lord and God. He will sup with you under the
tree and encourage you with His own speaking. He will

include you in His plans because you are His friend and He desires to invite you to share His heart in intercession.

---

1 1 Peter 2:11

2 Hebrews 11:10,14-16

3 Andrew Lamb pastors Acts 2 Church in Orlando, FL.

4 John 14:23 "Jesus answered and said to him, "If anyone loves Me, he will keep My word; and My Father will love him, and We will come to him and make Our abode with him."

5 Genesis 17:2 – the promise

6 Genesis 22 – the testing

CHAPTER SIX

INTO THE CLOUD

"A mystical touch is a deep, intimate contact-union-experience of God…it is not only a contact but also a union, and not only a union but also an experience."
-Thomas Dubay, S.M.

"In an instant my spirit was caught up into what seemed to be the next world. I saw an inaccessible light, and in this light what appeared like three sources of light, which I could not understand. And out of that light came words in the form of lightening which encircled heaven and earth. Out of the light came our dearly beloved Savior, unutterably beautiful with His shinning wounds and from this light came a voice."
-St. Maria Faustina Kowalska

INTO THE CLOUD

"He spoke to them in the pillar of cloud."
~*Psalm 99:7*

The Psalmist, quickened by the Spirit, has penned yet another Spiritual lesson for us upon whom the end of the ages has come.[1] God has hidden so much glorious revelation even in the most simple of Scriptures. As the Psalmist wrote, "For the commandment is a lamp and the teaching is light; and reproofs for discipline are the way of life."[2] The simple script of the books and letters of the Bible is the lamp that holds the light; it is not the light itself. The script written by the hands of the apostles and prophets had to have the inspiring light of the Spirit's fire inside of the lamp in order for it to quicken our souls even now in this dark age. As the Spirit's presence illuminates the simple words, He also enlightens us upon our way. Many times the illumination reproves us, showing our waywardness apart from Him; it also guides us, unveiling the route we must go, and teaches us the ways of God. May the light of the Spirit illumine these verses to not only enrich our understanding, but also quicken His life in us through His voice.

ADORATION

Starting in Psalms 99:5, we find a mystical spiritual itinerary describing the stages of progression of the soul's journey into God. As with all progress in the Spirit, this itinerary is sandwiched in adoration: the surrendered soul lovingly turning its wholehearted attention and affection, toward God in worshipful obedience. This is the foundation and crown of all experiential union with God.

THE CLOUD

The other day I was on my way to an early morning prayer meeting, passing through the city at about 5:00 AM. The clouds were so low, that at a particular section of the highway I entered the fog. When I was in this cloud, I could only see what was directly in front of me, illuminated by the beam of my headlights. If I had not seen the city before I entered the cloud, there would have been no way to know that I was even in the city. It didn't matter how high the buildings were or how many of them there were — I was blinded to their existence by the cloud. Of course, this did not mean that the buildings were no longer there, but they were invisible to me while I drove through the cloud. This is a great parallel of the life we can live in the presence of the Spirit: when we enter His presence (the cloud), we are blinded to the multiple massive earthly structures towering over us; in the cloud we are shrouded with Him and cannot see the cares of the world, the oppression of the authorities, the monetary system, the lusts of this life, the strivings of human nature; all is swallowed by the cloud.

The psalmist mentions three men in particular who chose to go into the cloud. They not only saw this cloud, as did the rest of the children of Israel, but actually entered into it. They gave themselves to the presence of God, casting all that they were, both positive and negative, into the cloud. Please do not read these next four words lightly: THEY CHOSE TO ENTER. Have you chosen to enter? It means leaving all other things behind in order to experience Him. This is the decision we must make: we must lay all other things aside or we won't be allowed to go inside.

The cloud is the manifestation of God's very person, His glory, His presence, and these men entered into it!

Moses, the most humble man upon the earth. Numbers 12:3 "Now the man Moses was very humble, more than any man who was on the face of the earth."

Aaron, "the spokesman." Exodus 7:1-2"Aaron shall be your prophet. You shall speak all that I command you, and your brother Aaron shall speak to Pharaoh..."

Samuel, the one who never had a word fall to the ground. 1 Samuel 3:19 "Thus Samuel grew and the LORD was with him and let none of his words fail."

MOSES

I wish to call your attention to the order in which these men are mentioned. Is it any wonder why Moses comes first? Humility is the foundation of all things erected by God, the vacuum by which we receive grace, the very image of God in man! To what else does God lend His merciful hand? In what other disposition does God chose to dwell? Humility is both rudimentary and paramount: without it there is no commencement of divine activity. The Cure d'Ars, a miracle-working lover of Jesus from 1800's France, wrote, "Without humility man only has the appearance of virtues." I am thoroughly convinced that God prefers an ounce of humility to a ton of talent and gifts.

AARON

Aaron, the spokesman, is connected to the humility that Moses represents; through this we see that the Aaron's speaking must walk side by side with Moses' humility. Speaking for God and humility to God is inseparably related — humility is the brother of the oracles of God. There is no spokesman who can stand without humility, for everything he says comes from humility. A spokesman that does not come from humility does not originate from God. Humility enters the cloud and the spokesman speaks what he received from the cloud: Moses went into the cloud to directly hear God's heart; Aaron entered the cloud to receive the message he would later deliver. If a spokesman tries to enter the cloud without being led by humility, he will not hear what he is to say because the oracle comes to humility for the spokesman to deliver. Aaron's job was to communicate what God installed in Moses and his powerful speaking came from Moses' humble hearing.

We must speak the things that God has said; as His spokesman in the earth we are the voice of the Most High in the world. Entering into the presence of God with humility is the origin of all our declaration. We enter the presence in humility and hear what we are to carry to God's people and the world. When John the Baptist was asked who he was, he said "I am a voice..." claiming no identity in himself. He was not selfishly invested in his own existence at all but was consumed by hearing, proclaiming, and preparing for God's Word. Like John, the spokesman completely gives himself over to listening, always mindful that everything he is depends upon hearing God.

SAMUEL

Samuel represents the last stage of those who enter the cloud. Samuel's words took on the unfailing quality of God's words simply because he only spoke God's pure words. As Madame Guyon wrote in her commentary on Exodus, "It is the property of God's speaking to absorb our own." Those who go into the cloud can be assured that not one of their words will fall to the ground simply because they are of one hundred percent divine origin. Samuel was unique among all the other prophets before and after him because he was both a priest and a prophet. He may be the only one of his kind, both ministering directly to the Lord in the Tabernacle *and* dispensing God's words to the world. Moses and Aaron become one in Samuel: humbly entering the presence of God and hearing God's Word in private, unashamedly speaking God's Word and executing God's will in public. Hebrews 11:32 states concerning Samuel: "Samuel and the prophets." A modern comparison could be "Jordan and the Bulls." Some have explained this passage saying, "Samuel was not exclusively a prophet." Samuel is singled out. Regardless of whether this is because he was a prophet among prophets or because he had both priestly and prophetic duties, he was an exceptional servant of God. He was not afraid to wield the sword and execute what others were religiously and politically afraid to, nor did he ever allow for partial obedience, severing himself from all allegiance to the world and its rulers. Samuel was ruthlessly and unyieldingly obedient to God.

OBEDIENCE

The humility of Moses received the word, the mouth of Aaron spoke the word and Samuel executed the word. These three kept the testimonies of the Lord and obeyed Him, painting a picture of the obedient life that results from entering and carrying the glory cloud. Some may disagree with this statement, but I believe that obedience to God is only possible when God emanates out of a man. When a man lays his life aside to enter into the presence of God and hear His voice, his own soul will be empowered with delight to do God's will. Jesus, the Word of God Himself, "delighted to do God's will."₃ Hearing the Word of God gives delight for obeying the will of God; power to fulfill God's will is found in receiving the Word of God itself.

OUTCOMES

What is so unique about these men? They are distinguished by the fact that when God invited them into the cloud, they entered in. They were swallowed by the cloud when they heard Him speak. This could be our distinction as well. If you are looking to hear God's sweet voice, it is most clearly heard in His sweet presence. Enter into His presence and stay there, saturated and soaked, perfumed and permeated with His person. John 1:1 says, "In the beginning was the Word and the Word was with God and the Word was God." Notice that the Word was "with God." The Word is in God's presence. Remember in Exodus 34 the reason why Moses' face shone: a shining face is connected with receiving God's voice.

Another result of entering the cloud is that they were heard or answered by the Lord. 1 John says, "And if we know that He hears us in whatever we ask, we know that we have the requests which we have asked from Him." John also records Jesus telling us that when we abide in Him, we receive answers to prayer.4 "If you abide in Me, and My words abide in you, ask whatever you wish, and it will be done for you." God answers the life that abides and lingers in the cloud of His presence.

Moses, Aaron and Samuel also received priceless forgiveness from the Lord. When you enter the presence of the Lord, you repent because you turn your attention from yourself to Him. His presence has a wonderful way of washing us and calling us to renounce all the things with which we burden ourselves. 1 John 1 says that fellowship with God is "the light" and they that walk in that fellowship are "cleansed from all sin," as if the light itself is the disinfectant. I have seen some people fall into the life of sin because they would not enter the presence of the Lord with their failures, but rather held on to their failures and cut themselves off from God.

Brothers and sisters, take your sin, shame, and failure into the cloud and you will find mercy. Keep it to yourself, distant from His presence, and you will shrivel like a plant without water or a branch detached from the vine.

A MAN IN THE PRESENCE OF GOD

One time I was with an elderly minister in his house; as soon as he began to direct his attention to the Lord in prayer, the room's atmosphere completely changed. It was as if God turned toward the room and gave His full attention to the sound of this man's voice. I was amazed at God's tangible response to this pastor's reverent address. I have never forgotten that moment and am continuously challenged to have God's ear as this saint did.

Now you may say, "We all have God's ear" and this is true, however there is a deeper level of response from the Lord that comes to those who remain in Him. For instance, Martha said the very same phrase to Jesus as Mary did, and Jesus responded in words of comfort; when Mary said the very same thing, the Lord responded in resurrection power. Did Jesus ignore Martha? No, absolutely not. He loved Martha, but Mary was a remarkably uncommon individual who stayed at Jesus feet.[6] As Martha served Mary stared. She humbly sat in His presence listening to His every word. She stayed in the cloud.

CONCLUSION

These men in Psalm 99, Moses (Humility), Aaron (Speaking) and Samuel (No Compromise) went into the cloud and were answered by God. Be assured that the one who lives in humility, enters the cloud of God in adoration, and listens to the voice of God will be infused with a delight to do God's will, steward God's words into the earth, ruthlessly obey, and possess the inclined ear of the Lord

CHAPTER SEVEN

THE GAZE
OF THE SOUL

"Waiting for God means power to do nothing save under command."
-G. Campbell Morgan

"To wait on God is to live a life of delight in God, as the lover waits on His beloved. Desire is love in motion; delight is love at rest. We must never wish for more than God. In Him we must be entirely satisfied; let Him be mine and I have enough. The gracious soul that dwells in God, is at home in Him, and there he dwells at ease."
-Matthew Henry

"Waiting! Yes, quietly waiting! No need for anxious dread; Shall He not assuredly guide me, Who gives me daily bread? Waiting! Yes, hopefully waiting! With hope that need not grow dim; The Master is pledged to guide me, and my eyes are unto Him."
-J.D. Smith

THE GAZE OF THE SOUL

"To You, I lift up my soul."
~Psalm 25:1

The prophetic poet paints upon the canvas of our minds once more with one of the most beautiful ballads known to man. He writes, "To You, oh Lord, I lift up my soul," revealing his soul's paramount yearning to completely fix itself upon God alone. Lifting up the soul to God means that the will presses the mind and affections upon God alone; the will of man abandons itself along with its faculties of reason and emotion entirely unto God. The soul's melody becomes: "I give you all the concentration of my mind and all the attentiveness of my heart that I have. I lift my gaze above the earth's futility and fasten it upon Your magnificence, relinquishing all of my affections to You. You are the object of my affections, and I give You all of my love, plunging myself irrevocably into Your care."

THE MIND OF MAN

The mind finds rest and illumination in the bliss of God's presence that comes through surrendering itself to God. David absolutely entrusts his past, present, and future to God when He writes, "in You I trust." The totality of His being trusts in God. Have you released your dreadful past to God or does your heart harbor its residue? Have you given your questions about the future to God or does fear keep your soul in confusion? What about today, this moment, even as you read these words: do you live as an abandoned adorer caught up in the Wind of the Spirit, or is your life scattered and tossed by your circumstances, like 1,000 sheets of paper blown every which way across an open field? Your present state is most important, for from it flows the power to release the past and future to God. It is an incredible understanding that the presence of the Lord is only in the present, which means we must presently relinquish ourselves into His presence.

The third verse reveals to us what David is describing: *a life of waiting upon God.* It reads, "...those who wait on You..." Drawing from the sequence of this artistic chronicle, the Spirit teaches us that to wait on the Lord is to lift up our soul to Him, to release ourselves to Him in absolute trust, and to sustain our adoring gaze upon Him. And the promise remains, "none of those who wait for You will be ashamed." What God-confidence this trusting life possesses! God-confidence comes from waiting upon God. The soul that chooses to lift itself up to God and release itself to trust in unrelenting adoration is free from ever being ashamed. Oh friends, we must learn to wait upon God. We must understand what it means, what it implies and what it performs in us. Men are looking everywhere to remove their fears; waiting on God is the only place where we can be assured that we will never be put to shame.

WAITING

Waiting is not postponing your initiative but putting it to death. I submit to you that waiting is centered on the presence of Christ, along with everything else in the Christian life. The bliss of His presence is the foundation for endurance in waiting upon God. Without His presence you will get tired of waiting, because we must understand that we do not wait *for* His presence, but *in* His presence. The picture that Isaiah 40 gives us of the one who waits is of one who has wind under his wings. Waiting is mounting up on the wind, specifically, soaring in the presence of the Spirit. The sweet bliss of His presence is found in the realm of waiting.

Subjectivity to the movement of the Spirit necessitates awareness of His presence. The problem is that we have trusted our own minds and leaned upon our own understanding. We have failed to abandon everything to Him. Even our very own intelligence must be offered up to Him, for when we fail to do this, we fail to make His presence the center of our lives. I am not writing about ministry, but rather our daily living. I am not just writing about our solitude with Him, but even our menial tasks. The blissful presence of the Spirit is not a part of the Christian life; it is both the whole of the Christian and that which makes the Christian whole. We must recognize that without the presence of the Lord, everything is dead and empty. In fact whenever His presence is not the center, we indirectly believe that our own understanding is of greater significance than the direction of His Spirit. Whenever His presence is not the center, we indirectly trust more in our human resolve than in His empowering presence. We must recognize our own frailty and exchange human resolve for the Spirit's quickening power. Only the Spirit gives life. Everything must issue out of His presence, and anything that doesn't come out of His presence is not from Him. One minister has said, "Whatever God doesn't initiate, He doesn't appreciate."

WAITING AND REVELATION

Waiting upon God is the source of revelation, the spiritual installation of the knowledge of God. Directly after the statement about waiting upon the Lord, the Psalmist writes, "make me know," "teach me," and "lead me." When a man chooses to wait upon God, he enrolls in the class of the Divine Teacher. The classroom where the Holy Teacher unfolds spiritual knowledge about the ways of the Kingdom and joyfully instructs the children about the reality of God's glorious person is in no other place than waiting upon God.

The waiting life will never be put to shame for God teaches this life Himself. The one who waits will receive revelation knowledge, because God will reveal Himself to him, not only installing it in him but also performing it through him.

Some years ago, Brian Guerin₁, a good friend and an incredible lover of Jesus, once told me, "Jesus is so revelatory that we receive revelation simply by His nearness." Friends, as we wait on God, God Himself will lead us. Daniel Kolenda₂ said an amazing statement concerning God and Abraham: "The reason why God did not tell Abraham where he was going was because He did not merely want to send Abraham to the promise land, He wanted to lead Him." One thing we must realize about God is that He chooses to hinge everything upon relationship with Him. He has made it so that we need Him to do everything, because He longs not only to be involved in everything but to perform everything in and through us. God will walk the path before us and He will internally guide us along the way as we wait in His presence. I know that I said this about two paragraphs ago, but it is so essential that I will write it again: *we do not wait for His presence, but rather we wait in His presence.* To disconnect from the reality of His presence is to not wait upon Him. Waiting is subjective to His presence.

WAITING IS SALVATION

The songwriter teaches that waiting in God's presence is salvation. Have you ever thought of it like that? Consider this: we have been saved from a wayward and wandering life — dark, oblivious, guideless. Submitted in His presence, we are now able to both listen to and hear our Guide; as we wait on Him we receive from Him. We are saved from a life separated from the Father, from a life without a teacher.

Yesterday, when I was in Wal-Mart, I saw on the front page of the newspaper that scientists have developed a magnetic treatment that helps reduce depression. This is ridiculous: depression is not an issue of the body but an issue of the soul. There is not a natural magnetic force that can pull depression out of the soul of man, but Christ not only draws *all* men, but *all of* the man into Himself. He pulls all of man's dreams and desires into Himself; even our spiritual, physical and soul ailments are reduced to nothing next to His magnetic mesmerizing vacuum as we wait in His presence and lift our souls to Him. Waiting upon God is both our salvation and life.

HUMILITY WAITS

In verse nine we see the Guide again. Not only does He go before us, but He reveals that the waiting life is a humble life, showing that waiting and humility are united. He leads the humble and teaches the humble.₃ In verse five, the Psalmist reveals his life disposition: "for you I wait all the day." It is not waiting *until*, but rather, just…waiting. This kind of waiting transcends reason, frustrating the mind, for waiting by its earthly definition is other than this endless subjectivity. The world waits until something happens; we wait as a fixed internal disposition. We are to live in this state of subjectivity to Him, for throughout the day, we wait. To wait is to be led, and even as you are led, you are waiting.

WAITING AND INTIMACY

Verse 12 shows us that waiting and humility have another sibling, or perhaps another manifestation: "Who is the man who fears the Lord? God will instruct him in the way he should choose." Looking at verse twelve, together with verses four, five, and nine, we see the union of humility, waiting, and the fear of the Lord. Not only is this soul prosperous, fruitful and abundant in life, but above all, she is granted access into the intimate chambers of the bridegroom. In sequence, the Psalmist teaches us that the waiting, humble and God fearing soul receives intimate revelation. "The intimacy of the Lord is for those who fear Him and He will make them know..." Intimacy and revelation are united again. We must recognize that these things — the presence of God, intimacy, revelation, humility, the fear of the Lord, waiting on God — are inseparable. Intimacy with God is reserved for those who fear, for those who wait, for those who are humble. If a man does not wait he does not fear God. Does this make sense to you? Does it bother you? Pride will move on without God. But the Psalmist reveals the simple secret to the humble waiting life that fears the Lord by taking us full circle to the beginning ("to you oh Lord I lift up my soul") with verse 15: "My eyes are continually toward the Lord." He is continually waiting, continually submitted, continually seeing, continually fearful and continually intimate. And though there are many trials and tribulations in his life, he looks to the Lord to be gracious and to pardon his iniquity as his heart is set to obey.

THE SETTING OF THE HEART

The setting of the heart is imperative. In Psalm 112:7, the Scriptures show that the righteous man has *fixed his heart* to trust in God, which means this righteous man will not change his mind as he is anchored and immovable. In the next verse, David states that he has established his heart, demonstrating that his heart is set and ordered. The fixing of the heart causes the setting of the heart, resulting in fearless living: the established heart is fixed and fearless. The heart is the nucleus of the human body, pumping life through the veins and providing all that is needed for life. If the heart stops, life ends. But the heart also represents affections. Can there be love without affections? We are to love the Lord with our whole heart, deeply and affectionately connected to Jesus. St. Augustine spoke of "setting love in order," believing that all sin and disobedience was a result of an disordered love. Jesus told us that all thoughts proceed from the heart. So the fixing of the heart is the establishing or ordering of the whole man.

DEPENDENCY

King David concludes this exposition on the waiting humble life by stating his dependency: "guard my soul." His meek heart confesses that he cannot even guard himself. This is surely one of the main reasons he was a man after God's own heart. I immediately think of Psalm 16:1 where he again voices such dependency upon God: "Preserve me; in you I place my trust." I need You to guard me. In my own heart, I cry, "Deliver me, for I cannot deliver myself. Do not let me be ashamed because I take refuge in you." No one who waits upon God will be put to shame. The one who continually looks unto God and waits on Him all day, who lifts up his soul to the Lord in trust and adoration and humility, who listens to the Lord and enjoys sweet intimacy with Him — this one lives in the refuge of God. Confidently, the son of Jesse drafts, "I take refuge in You."

CONCLUSION

The Psalmist ties together the preserved life with an upright life, lived in integrity through waiting upon God: "let integrity and uprightness preserve me, for I wait for you." He begins by lifting up His soul and concludes with waiting. I believe that the His first phrase, "To you I lift up my soul" and His last phrase, "I wait for you" are explanations of one another and every verse in between is an expounding on the same.

Friend, waiting upon God is the true posture of the soul that is lifted up to the Lord. Only lifting your soul up to God is waiting upon the Lord. All around us, people are confused and hurt, unstable, broken and wounded. All over the world people's minds and emotions speed through the highways of life, unable to stop recklessly destroying themselves and others. But we who believe on the Lord Jesus Christ are drawn into His beauty by lifting up our souls to Him and mounting up over the efforts and chaos of the earth; as men with wings of eagles, we wait upon Him.

---

1 Brian Guerin leads a ministry called Bridal Glory.

2 Daniel Kolenda, current operating director of Christ for All Nations (CFAN), was speaking to me about his book, Live Before You Die, when he gave this statement.

3 Proverbs 11:3 "With the humble is wisdom."

CHAPTER EIGHT

OBEY

"One act of obedience is better than 100 sermons."
-Dietrich Bonheoffer

"A solider will obey His master even unto death and I cannot look Christ in the face and obey Him any less than a solider His master."
-Praying Hyde

"To obey is better than sacrifice, I don't need you money, I want your life."
-Keith Green

"There is no substitute for prayer and obedience."
-Leonard Ravenhill

"If you love Me you will obey me."
-Jesus the Christ

OBEY

"Whatsoever He saith unto you, do it."
~John 2:5 KJV

As the wedding went on, the wine ran out. Mary says to the servants, "whatsoever He saith unto you do it." As they obeyed they saw the glory of God. Herein lies the heart of manifesting the glory God, namely, obedience.

WHATSOEVER

Mary reveals the first element of obedience: the word "whatsoever." Dear reader, I eagerly await the day that "whatsoever" returns into the heart of Christianity. David Brainerd wrote, "I care not where I live, how I live or what hardships I may go through that I may but gain souls to Christ." Though it is far from the convenient Christianity in the West today, God loves the "whatsoever." I remember Dr. Michael L. Brown saying concerning our preferences for (or against) missions, "Are we going to let people go to hell because we don't like the menu?"[1] I'll never forget when I heard K. P. Yohannan speak about the realization that changed the whole course of his life: "If hell is real, I must do something more than what I am currently doing in my life."[2] Because of this insight, he sold his castle of a home and moved to the slums of India to give his life to the poor. C.T. Studd wrote a booklet called, "Don't Care a Damn Christians." He called them D.C.D.'s. In modern language, that booklet today would be called "Don't Give a Damn Christians." He proposed that God is looking for men who care for nothing but Christ and His gospel.

Is your life this way? Is there a "whatsoever" in your heart? Can you honestly say, "Lord Jesus, wherever, whenever and whatever you wish from me I will do"? We must ask ourselves if our obedience is unconditional, for only in unconditional obedience is freedom. Are you free to do the will of God or are you bound by the tyranny of self, cluttered by things of this world? Friend, you are compromised to the degree that you cannot leap at Christ's first mention of your name.

Hesitance manifests doubt and mistrust, but God seeks faith and trust in Him that advances at His slightest whisper, even without knowing exactly where to go. He desires a life that will not shrink back. "If my righteous one shrinks back I will not be pleased with Him."[3] When the "whatsoever" flows through your veins, you possess one of the greatest exhilarations in life: the freedom to express God infinitely. You possess liberty from that tyrant who rules the world along with many Western Christians: self-will. Joy beams from the face of one who is clean from the mud of hesitation and free from the shackles of fear. Reader, I ask you again, do you have a "whatsoever" in your heart for God?

HE SAYS

The second element of obedience that Mary speaks is this: "He saith." As important as it is to abandon yourself to God's "whatsoever," it is aimless without knowing what "He saith." The directive must originate in Him — God speaks and His sheep hear His voice. The "whatsoever" must stand upon what "He saith" or we are in danger of merely seeking the thrill or living for the cause. Many go to great lengths and seek with all their might to please God, possibly much farther than you or I have, yet they do not know Him because they don't hear His voice. We cannot be driven by a cause or even morality alone because we don't just have a cause, we have

Christ. Followers of Christ are abandoned to Christ. He speaks and we obey His voice.

It is imperative to hear, for hearing is the way to righteousness. Abraham heard the word and obeyed it; his obedience to the word was credited to him as righteousness. Righteousness comes when the word that enters a man by hearing exits a man through obedience. To hear and obey is our only hope. Again, this aligns itself with God's loving nature who desires that everything hinges upon interactive fellowship with Him. My friend, do you hear Him?

Maybe the whatsoever already burns deep in your heart and your soul screams, "ANYTHING LORD! I WILL DO ANYTHING YOU WISH!" After the initial encounter many become just like Paul: when the light of Christ surrounds him, blinds him, and knocks him to the ground, the initial response from his repentant heart is, "Who are you Lord and what would you have me do?" Paul's encounter with Christ caused him to say, "I want to know you and I will do anything you wish," but it is imperative to do just as Paul did and do exactly what God says, for without obedience to God's specific speaking, we will rush off abandoned to God's will yet still blind to God's specific instructions. Because Paul obeyed God, his eyes were opened to see how he could give his life in faithful obedience and meet his insatiable thirst for God's will.

UNTO YOU

The third element of obedience that Mary says to the servant is, "unto you." It is imperative that we recognize that God's speaking is utterly personal. He speaks "unto you." What He speaks to me is not what He speaks to another. This saves us tremendously from performance and competition. We all should hear His personal voice; what is He saying directly to you? He calls His sheep *by their names.*₄ They do not follow Him merely because they know His voice, but because He speaks to them individually as well.

I want you to take a moment, close your eyes, and recollect the last thing that God has placed upon your heart to do, whether it is grand or small. Do you remember it? If you can, think about what stopped you from doing it. I guarantee that its impediment was either self-awareness or self-preservation of some kind. The value of His voice must be greater than the value of our own face. John Tauler wrote in *Sermons and Conferences*, "The light of faith transcends the scope of its own reason." His voice trumps my mind. Sister Mary of the Holy Trinity said, "Faith is the submission of the mind."₅ We must truly trust in the Lord with all our hearts and lean not on our own understanding. Maybe as you read this you say to yourself, "I don't think I have heard anything." Sister Mary also wrote from the Lord, "Why do you not hear my call? Have I not exhausted every means to beg your attention..."₆ Friends, we must realize that we are not only held accountable for what we have heard, but also for what we should have heard but couldn't because we weren't listening. We must hear Him. My friend David Popovici₇ spoke to me about three things that are most important in hearing God's voice:

"You must believe that God speaks and that He will reward those who would diligently seek Him with more of His voice. One has to believe that God is a speaking God. Islam says that God speaks no more. Many people don't believe that God speaks. If they do believe He speaks, they don't believe that He speaks in a very consistent way, or even that He wants to speak. So we must have faith that God speaks. One must be looking to Him and believing that He wants to speak. Number two: men need humility to recognize his deep need for the voice of God. He should feel that if God does not speak he cannot live. If I cannot hear Him I don't want to live. Without His voice I cannot exist. Real poverty of Spirit, and deep consciousness for my need for His voice above all. Lastly, purity of heart. For the pure in heart will see God. You can equate seeing God with hearing God or God's communicating Himself to man."

We must hear what He has to say to us, personally. We must abandon ourselves in order to dive into God's will revealed through His voice.

DO IT

"Whatsoever He saith unto you...DO IT" The last part is to simply do it. Listen: this little article can actually shift your whole life if you will allow its voice to revive your abandonment to obedience, not matter what the cost. He is so worth it; His voice is life and obedience to it is everything. To obey His voice is more valuable to God than all the sacrifices and benevolent actions in the entire world. Allow His speaking to permeate your heart and inspire your being into perfect synchronization with Him. God's voice carries within itself the ability to perform the very thing He requires you to do. Jesus said in John 12:50 (NIV), "I know that my Father's command...is life." In other words, He tells me that I am enabled with His very own life to carry out His command. All you need is for God to speak to you and to abandon yourself to His speaking; then it will work into who you are and living it out will come naturally. This is the only way to "do it."

SERVANTHOOD

Mary gave this command to servants. A servant is someone who lives to meet the needs of another. Before there can truly be a "whatsoever," we must first resolve in our hearts that we no longer live for ourselves. "And He died for all, so that they who live might no longer live for themselves, but for Him who died and rose again on their behalf" (2 Corinthians 5:15). After these servants, who already lived to supply the needs of their master, [1]recognized their lack of wine, [2]heard the command, and [3]obeyed all that Jesus said to them, Jesus manifested His glory and miraculously turned the water to wine.

Just as a side note, Jesus told the servants to fill empty jars. Here we have a picture of the life that has been miraculously turned from ordinary water to divine wine in the jars that were used. They started empty so that they could be totally filled, to the brim. We see that in order for a life to be turned to wine, it must be empty of self and filled with obedience. When the world drinks this life they will receive the manifestation of the glory of the Son and the intoxicating love of God.

CONCLUSION

One time, while Reinhard Bonnke was preaching about the key that opened Africa to the Gospel, I asked the Lord about what key would unlock America; I felt deep in my heart that the key to awakening America is wine, namely, the experience of the Spirit. If this is true, the glory of the Lord will only manifest when a servant abandons his life so completely to the specific speaking of God that he obeys God in whatever He wishes. Jesus said, "*Glorify me that I might glorify you.*" God invested His glory into the Son, and through His obedience, the Son returned that glory back to the Father through utterly abandoning Himself to God's will. Jesus prayed, "...not my will but Yours be done." There is no glory to God in a life lived for itself. The prerequisite for giving glory to God is to give ourselves completely to Him. *"Whatsoever He saith unto you, do it."*

---

1 Dr. Michael L. Brown, Called To Die message preached in Brownsville Assembly of God in 1999

2 K.P. Yohannan Christ's Call To Follow In His Footsteps audio message from www.sermonindex.com

3 Hebrews 10:38

4 John 10:3

5 Sister Mary of the Trinity, *Words of Love* (Rockford, Ill: TAN books and Publishers, 1985) p. 21.

6 Trinity, p. 5.

7 David Popovici is the founder of Kingdom Gospel Mission.

CHAPTER NINE

AM I NOT MORE TO YOU THAN TEN SONS

"He who delights in the possession of the Lord Jesus has all that heart can wish. As for 'created things', they are like shallow and deceitful brooks — they fail to supply our needs, much less our wishes. The creature without Christ is an empty thing, a lamp without oil, a bone without marrow. But when Christ is present, our cup runs over, and we eat bread to the full. A dinner of herbs, when we have communion with Him, is as rich a feast as a stalled ox; and our narrow cot is as noble a mansion as the great house of the wealthy. Go not abroad, you hungry wishes of my soul — stay at home, and feast on Jesus; for abroad you must starve, since all other beloveds are empty and undesirable. Stay with Christ, and eat that which is good, and delight yourself in fatness."

-Charles Spurgeon

AM I NOT MORE TO YOU THAN TEN SONS

"Am I not more to you than ten sons."
~1 Samuel 1:8

[1.]Now there was a certain man from Ramathaim-zophim from the hill country of Ephraim, and his name was Elkanah...[2.]He had two wives: the name of one was Hannah and the name of the other Peninnah; and Peninnah had children, but Hannah had no children. [3.]Now this man would go up from his city yearly to worship and to sacrifice to the LORD of hosts in Shiloh... [4.]When the day came that Elkanah sacrificed, he would give portions to Peninnah his wife and to all her sons and her daughters; [5.]but to Hannah he would give a double portion, for he loved Hannah, but the LORD had closed her womb. [6.]Her rival, however, would provoke her bitterly to irritate her, because the LORD had closed her womb. [7.]It happened year after year, as often as she went up to the house of the LORD, she would provoke her; so she wept and would not eat. [8.]Then Elkanah her husband said to her, "Hannah, why do you weep and why do you not eat and why is your heart sad? Am I not better to you than ten sons?" [9.]Then Hannah rose after eating and drinking in Shiloh. Now Eli the priest was sitting on the seat by the doorpost of the temple of the LORD. [10.]She, greatly distressed, prayed to the LORD and wept bitterly. [11.]She made a vow and said, "O LORD of hosts, if You will indeed look on the affliction of Your maidservant and remember me, and not forget Your maidservant, but will give Your maidservant a son, then I will give him to the LORD all the days of his life, and a razor shall never come on his head."
(1 Samuel 1:1-11)

In the day and culture in which Elkanah and Hannah lived, a woman found her identity and dignity in bearing children. Her main role was to give her husband children, especially a son to carry on the father's name and line. The fruitfulness of her womb was the culture's only measure of success and value for a woman. Elkanah's other wife, Peninnah, had a fruitful womb. Her "production" testified to her culture that she was a successful wife, and her "productivity" was her confidence. Having many children awarded her dignity, identity and praise, removing the pressure of the culture's thought patterns off of her shoulders; her fruitfulness gave evidence as a prideful witness that she had proven herself in accordance with her culture.

HANNAH

Hannah on the other hand, though she was greatly loved, was barren and had the pressure of the culture constantly weighing down on her. Obviously, the provocative testimony of the other wife was internally vexing, degrading and humiliating; Hannah suffered such emotional pressure and humiliation that she was sick to her stomach and could not eat. The mindset of the culture demanded that she produce something that she was simply unable to. This constant tension broke her soul: she was distraught and oppressed by the cultural traditions, but most of all, Hannah was shamed by Peninnah's fruitful life. Peninnah provoked her, but the power she had over Hannah did not come from Peninnah herself, but rather from the patterns of thinking in their culture. Ultimately, Hannah was oppressed by the voice of human demand, human systems, and human traditions.

Do you relate to Hannah? Are you depressed and frustrated with your ministry, judging its success by the numbers (of salvations, of healings, of responses) or results? Are you burdened because your ministry is not growing or frustrated because the unsaved haven't submitted to the Gospel through your witness? If there is any competition hidden in your veins, or any jealousy harbored in your soul, keep reading. I promise that Jesus will eradicate it through one phrase.

ELKANAH AND JESUS

When Hannah comes to her husband, he gives the greatest portrayal of the heart of Jesus Christ that there could be in this situation by saying, "Am I not more to you than ten sons?" It is almost as if he was hurt by the fact that something else was the measure of her life.

These words reveal to us that, in his great love for her, he looked for the reason why she was not fulfilled by his love alone. He asks her, "Am I not of more value to you than many children?" Ten is a great number because it represents completion, and as stated earlier, sons are the greatest fruit a woman can have. Elkanah is asking his oppressed wife in her frustration, "Am I not more to you than all the fruit in the world?" My dear friend, this is the heart of Jesus. In the same way, He asks: "Are you not fulfilled in me? Am I not enough? Am I not all sufficient? Am I not I AM? Is fruit (results) more precious to you than I am? Why do you need something more than me to be happy, satisfied or delighted? My heart hurts because you are not fulfilled by my love." I believe some of our frustrated prayers break God's heart, for they reveal to Him that He is no longer the center of our hearts. Jesus' heart is broken by much of our ambition for results, for it replaces Him as the source and joy of life. To be loved by you is the goal of His loving you.

Elkanah gives Hannah such a shocking love that exists outside the thought processes of man. His love finds value in her without demanding fruitfulness as the culture does; his love wants her to be satisfied only with him; in his love, the couple needs nothing more than each other.

HANNAH'S ALTERATION

In response to such a loving statement from her husband that proved he only wanted her for herself, she stopped weeping, got up, found her appetite and *communed with her husband at the table*. The sad fact is that much of our crying for fruit has robbed us of sweet communion with Jesus. And though in the next verse she again cries for fruitfulness, her tears are different; we find a subtle change that makes all the difference in the entire world. She still pleads for a son, the best fruit, but now it is for a totally different reason. Her motive is changed and purified. While her first cries came from the painful weight of the system of man that wrapped her identity and dignity in productivity and fruitfulness, her last cry is simply to have fruit to be able to give to God. She wants to bear the best fruit to be able to offer at the feet of God Himself. She is no longer bound by thinking of her own face and testifying of her own life in accordance with the system of the culture, speaking man's language of success, beating herself for lack of fruit and comparing her life to others. Now she is free to find all her joy in her husband and not worry if he will leave her if she is unable to produce; now she cries to God for the right reason, lifting up her tears in purity and weeping out of selflessness. She no longer wants fruit to validate herself; she wants fruit to present to God, to give something of value to Him instead of seeking to be valued by her culture.

GOD'S PURIFICATION

One may say, "The scripture stated earlier that God had closed her womb, so her fruitlessness was because of God."

Exactly! Sometimes God prevents us from bearing the fruit that *we* want so that He can look into our eyes and say, "Am I not more to you than ten sons?" When God spoke this to me personally, He broke me out of a bondage that I didn't even know I was in, breaking me into a realm of freedom, rest, and ease beyond anything I could have ever thought possible, a realm where the literal joy of heaven and the wine of the Spirit could be consumed for the right reason — intimate union. A preacher who is looking for more signs and wonders; a pastor who wants a building; an evangelist who desires to see more numbers; a teacher who wants more committed students — whatever your frustration for productivity might be, in your frustration listen to the heart of your Bridegroom, for it beats with this lovely phrase, "Am I not more to you than those things? Am I not enough for you? Am I not more to you than a building? Am I not more to you than miracles? Am I not more to you than souls being saved? Am I not more to you than apparent fruitfulness?"

This issue must be settled first: if we are ever to pray with a pure cry, we must be satisfied with Him alone. If we ever want to be pure enough to simply desire to lay fruit at His feet, we must find such contentment with His simple love and presence, forsaking the longings for our own significance. This issue of being satisfied with God alone will open up our hearts to offer to Jesus our substance. Hannah says, "I will give him to you all the days of his life." Her heart cries, "This fruit is not for my name, no one will even see me with him. This fruit is not to remove my disgrace and shame or to give me dignity or identity...it is all for You, and You alone." We will be forever set free from the oppressive demand for production when we settle in our hearts that Jesus alone in our lives and daily experience is enough to satisfy everything that we could ever desire. He is enough!

SAMUEL

Brothers and sisters, we must return to first love: love that is solely set upon Him alone and satisfied with Him alone, so that fruit can be exactly what it is supposed to be — the work of God, performed by God and offered to God for God alone. May we never fall into the trap of finding our identity and dignity in how much we have done and can do for the Lord, or how much God has used us, because the real issue is this: if He Himself is not enough, your fruit will be tainted because it was not conceived out of the purity of satisfaction with God alone — you will never birth a Samuel into the world. Penninah's children were just regular kids that you never hear anything else about; their names, lives, and works perished with them. But Samuel was set apart — he was a loyal prophet and burning priest unlike any other; his words never fell to the ground; there is no other prophet-priest like Samuel except for Jesus Himself. His life is a picture of enduring supernatural work and an exposition of the everlasting effects that will accompany the life satisfied with God alone; he represents the eternal impact of a life in love with the Bridegroom. In Hebrews the author writes, "...Samuel and the prophets..." indicating that Samuel was significant in all the records of time. He stood out from those who stood out and shone above those who shone.

Significant fruit like Samuel is born only after the question is settled and we can say with all our hearts, "You yourself are more to me than all the fruit and success in the world. If I have everything and I don't have you, I have nothing, but If I have You and nothing else in the world, I have everything." Join me in praying: *"JESUS, YOU ARE MORE THAN ENOUGH FOR ME AND MY DESIRE FOR FRUIT IS ONLY TO HAVE AN OFFERING TO LAY AT YOUR FEET."*

-CHAPTER TEN-

THE SHEPHERDSHIP

The LORD is my shepherd; I shall not want. He maketh me to lie down in green pastures: he leadeth me beside the still waters. He restoreth my soul: he leadeth me in the paths of righteousness for his name's sake. Yea, though I walk through the valley of the shadow of death, I will fear no evil: for thou art with me; thy rod and thy staff they comfort me. Thou preparest a table before me in the presence of mine enemies: thou anointest my head with oil; my cup runneth over. Surely goodness and mercy shall follow me all the days of my life: and I will dwell in the house of the LORD for ever.

-Psalm 23 KJV

SHEPHERDSHIP

"The Lord is my Shepherd..."
~Psalm 23:1

THE LORD IS MY SHEPHERD

What does this phrase mean: "The Lord is my Shepherd"? It simply tells us that the Shepherd is the Lord and the Lord is the Shepherd. It is important to note that someone cannot claim the bountiful benefits of His shepherd-ship until he or she is submitted to His Lordship. The Lord is the Ruler and King, the Manager and Master. Jesus said in Luke 6:46, "Why do you call me, 'Lord, Lord' and do not do what I say?" Lordship is intimately connected with obedience to His voice, and means that you no longer live for yourself; it means that you recognize and align yourself with the truth that "you have been bought with a price;"₁ it means that you no longer call the shots because "you are not your own;"₂ it means that God has purchased your life, your heart, your decisions, your family, your dreams and plans for Himself. To call Him Lord is to relinquish all rights to yourself. Oswald Chambers once wrote, "The only right the Christian has is the right to give up his rights."

When someone accepts the Manager he or she comes under His management. Leonard Ravenhill once said, "The greatest sin in the world is not adultery; it is rather, 'I can manage my life without God.'" How did he come to that conclusion? There is a major difference between the fruit of sin and the root of sin. The fruits of sin are all the things done against God's law, but the root of sin is the inward rebellion to God's rule, which is self-life. Isaiah 53:6 tells us, "All we like sheep have gone astray, we all have gone our own way. But the

Lord has caused the iniquity of us all to fall on Him." Note that "going astray" in the first part of the verse is immediately expounded upon as "our own way." Waywardness is self-management. Our sin is nothing more than refusing to subject ourselves to God's divine rule. The last part of the verse is the good news: Jesus has taken upon Himself the bondage and death caused by the tyranny of self-rule for all who choose to place their trust in Him. Do you recognize why the Shepherd must be Lord and that only the Lord can be the Shepherd? Dear reader, it is simply because only under Lordship can Shepherd-ship be a reality.

Dr. Michael L. Brown said, "If there was a way for Jesus to be Savior and not Lord, then that would mean that He never dealt with the root issue in Eden." Adam's self-management was in direct disobedience to God's rule. How does Jesus handle Peter when he seeks to use the same tactics? The Master says, "Get behind Me, Satan! You are a stumbling block to Me; for you are not setting your mind on God's interests, but man's." In the same line of thought, can you recall *Jesus Discipleship 101*? "If any man would come after Me, let Him deny Himself, take up His cross and follow Me." Lordship must mean that He is the Lord of everyday and I give myself to obey whatever I hear Him say.

Now let me say our initial statement again: "The Lord is my Shepherd." If He is not your Lord, He is not your Shepherd. In other words, one cannot claim the beauty of His Shepherd-ship without the majesty of His Lordship. Submission to the Lordship of Christ rends the veil and invites us into a glorious world that would have otherwise remained unknown. Let us take a look inside.

I SHALL NOT WANT

Once a life is laid at His feet, it is in that very moment completely satisfied for the tender Shepherd is all that is needed. There is no need that the Good Shepherd cannot meet; all cravings are all filled in Him. Sheep in the presence of the Shepherd are free from the need to want anything else. Men cannot be satisfied while they look at all kinds of other things to escape from their loneliness, confusion, and despair; only in the Shepherd-ship of the Lord can men find satisfaction and say, "I have not a want in the world but God alone." The Scriptures tell us that those who seek the Lord lack no good thing.₃

Sin set in motion the selfish, vain cravings for self-gratification, scattering our souls into endless pursuits for things other than Him. But when God settles all the scattered, selfish vanity of our souls by calling us to take pleasure in Him, then all the aimless, defiled waywardness dissolves and men can once again bear the image of God. The issue of Christ-likeness is an issue of the soul being completely satisfied in God. The Psalmist clearly tells us that in the presence of the Shepherd we have not a care in the world, for in Him are all things. Psalm 73 says, "Besides you, I desire nothing on the earth." In its context of, this statement is written as result of being in the presence of God.

There is a story/poem about a stray sheep who makes his way to another flock and its Shepherd. When a couple of the sheep in the new flock see this stray sheep, lost and confused, hungry and tired, one turns to the other and says, "Do you see him there? I really want to know, why this confused sheep knows not where to go." The other sheep turns in reply, "It really must be, that he has not a Shepherd such as cares for you and me."

HE MAKES ME LIE DOWN IN GREEN PASTURES

Such a complete satisfaction in God that silences all the noisy cravings of the soul is only the diving board from which to jump into the rest of this glorious blissfully led life under the Shepherd, for the Psalmist tells us that when we submit to the Shepherd, He annihilates our covetous cravings and "makes us lie down in green pastures." The Lord gives rest. He requires that you come away from the hustle and bustle of life and rest in the pasture. He causes His own to rest, providing a place for them to lie down in safety and ease. So many rush and worry, strive and perform, all the while afraid and confused about what it even means to rest. My dear friend, when you experience one moment of rest in the presence of the Lord, you will be wonderfully unable to string any words together in an attempt to describe it. Do you lack rest? Come to the Shepherd and He will give it to you. Do you lack ease? Come to the Shepherd for His yoke is easy.

Along with rest, the Shepherd provides food in the pasture. It is in laying, at ease and at rest, that one receives the delightful nourishment from the pasture. To be submitted to the Shepherd is to know no want, to rest in ease, and to feast upon Him. Have you made the connection that the nourishment of the green pasture is linked together with the abundant life Christ unveils to us? In John 10:9-10 Jesus connects our abundant life with eating Him. Abundant life is contingent upon consuming Him. Witness Lee writes, "It is through fellowship that we enjoy the riches of divine life."

HE LEADS ME BESIDES THE STILL WATERS

The divine leadership of the Lord leads beside still waters. It is important to note that only the Shepherd leads us there; we cannot access this point by ourselves. The still waters are only accessed by divine guidance; He leads us to these waters both by His example before us and His presence with us. We find the still waters as a result of His leading.

The Shepherd keeps His sheep near water. There is no need for any to suffer thirst along the way for the journey is beside the waters. Dryness is a product of either taking a route that leads away from the Shepherd, or failing to avail yourself of the abundant nourishment.

What is the significance of the waters being still? The Hebrew wording for still waters is "waters of rests:" both the words "waters" and "rests" are plural. This is very interesting, for it points to the many uses of water, and each function of water leads to another experience of rest. The water is the quenching of your thirst *and* the washing of the word. The fact that His leadership is in close proximity to water reveals to us that He leads us hand in hand while quenching our thirst and washing us in the water of His word.

HE RESTORES MY SOUL

The soul is in great need of restoration and only Jesus, the good Shepherd, can restore it. The mind is constantly subject to the chaotic flow of the Adamic nature, but when our minds are stayed upon Him they remain at perfect peace.4 Our minds cannot find restoration in a systematic programming of the mind; only the Prince of Peace can restore the disorder of the mind. The efforts of men fall miserably short in setting a person's emotions free but the presence of Jesus can calm the raging sea with one word. It is imperative that the soul be restored from our forefather Adam's induced degeneration; this alone is the work of the life giving Spirit Himself.

HE GUIDES ME

All things move toward one goal, that is, the glory of God. Each work of the Lord, from planting to pruning to harvesting, is a matter of glorifying God. His guidance is for one end: His name's sake. The paths we travel are many, but each one is routed to the glory of God. No matter which you choose you will end at the glory of His name, and He guides you for His name sake. Those who lack guidance lack glory; those not led by God are not aligned with the glory of His name. May the name of Jesus be lifted high! How? By walking in His presence down the path that He Himself has chosen. Notice that it doesn't say "He guides us" but rather "He guides me." It is an individual and personal thing to be led by the Lord down His own path.

VALLEY OF THE SHADOW

Even though death's shadow is upon you in the valleys of this world, the Psalmist says, "You are with me." This is an absolute liberation from the slavery of fear! In this present moment of darkness, Christ's presence is your confidence. "I will not fear" is an amazing deliverance. Fear what? Death's power is worthless next to His presence; you don't have any fear when you fear God, but when you don't fear the Lord you are full of the spirit of fear. Many would say that the "valley of the shadow of death" is a place of abandonment or spiritual dryness, but it is nothing of the sort, for the presence of the Lord carries and delivers us from all fear, even the fear of death itself.

The next line says, "Your rod and Your staff, they comfort me." The rod is a symbol of protection and the staff is a symbol of direction. The Shepherd uses the rod to protect the sheep and beat off the wolves and he uses the staff to direct the herd by a corrective nudge on the face of any deviator. Dr. Michael L. Brown used to say, "I am much more confident in His ability to lead than my ability to follow." This is why the Psalmist is comforted by the rod and staff: not only will the Good Shepherd fiercely protect you from predators that seek to harm you, but He will keep you on the straight and narrow. "I will instruct you and teach you in the way you should go; I will counsel you with my eye upon you."₅

A TABLE

Because of God's call upon my life to bring the church into a deeper experience of the Life of God, I am constantly criticized as a "sunshine and rainbows" preacher. I have had ministers who are older, wiser, and more constant in the faith than myself come up to me and say, "Not everything is delightful in God," or (my favorite), "There is coming a day when God will leave you to yourself and the enemy, and there you will find out what you are truly made of." Perhaps they are right. At the time of this writing I am 17 years in the Lord, and maybe I am too young and naive to understand "abandonment" time. But all I know and preach is what God has shown me, and you cannot alter the fact that "He prepares a table before me in the presence of my enemies." No matter what surrounds me, I can have sweet communion with Him. If He had to leave me to test me, then that would mean that He is seeking to fashion me into something apart from Himself, apart from dependency on Him, apart from His empowering presence. I don't buy it. I need Him and the sweet meals He prepares for me right in front of an enormous army of devils salivating for my soul.

He has "anointed my head with oil," smearing His own substance upon me. The dripping of His oil and the fragrance of His ointment are continually upon me. Notice that the anointing follows the table; we eat of Him, receiving Him internally, and then He rests upon us externally. He expounds upon this with the next statement, "my cup runs over." I once heard an amazing man of God say that the presence of the Lord is internal while the anointing of the Lord is external. When the presence of the Lord fills the inner man, it will begin to spill over onto the outer man, just like a cup that is being filled when it overflows the sides and covers the outside. The Shepherd is so good! He lets us rest, drink, wash, eat, and then He overflows in us. The inflow creates an outflow which causes an overflow.

DWELL IN THE HOUSE

What confidence David has to say, "Surely goodness and mercy will follow me all the days of my life." The goodness and mercy of the Lord follow those who follow the Lord; they are only a product on the trail that the Good Shepherd leaves behind. David's confidence is not in His own reproduction of goodness but rather in the pursuing goodness and mercy of the Shepherd Himself. I believe David's last statement is the encapsulating phrase: "I will dwell in the house of the Lord forever." The dwelling place of God becomes the dwelling place of man as man surrenders to the Lordship of Christ. Abiding in the presence of the Lord is for the submitted sheep, and all the bountiful blessings of this glorious realm are the wonderful realities of God's own house. Rest, ease, satisfaction, nourishment, guidance, leadership, restoration, protection, direction, presence, anointing, filling, overflowing, goodness and mercy are the perks simply being a resident in the house of the Good Shepherd, and His leadership is found in the presence of the Lord.

---

1 1 Corinthians :20

2 1 Corinthians 6:19

3 Psalm 34:10

4 Isaiah 26:3

5 Psalm 32:8

Into The Cloud

CHAPTER ELEVEN

THE CROSS

As I see The God-man hanging there
With His bloody-matted hair
Sinners passing without a care
The Pharisees in satisfaction stare
And the soldiers gambling to take their share
He shivers and His palms tear
God bleeds and pain he bears
His cross planted between the pair
Naked He drips blood there
I am increasingly aware
Of the fairest love beyond compare

THE CROSS

The mind of man is free to fasten upon whatever it wishes, drawing happiness from pastimes or sorrow from memories, anger from hurts or joy from inspiration, but once the soul agrees to set its attention upon the suffering God-man, it passes into a quality of meditation beyond all others. This meditation actually shatters the iron rebellion in the will of man and softens the stony heart that is unable to yield to God. Nothing so exemplifies the wisdom, humility, and selfless love of the Father as much as the Son, who chose to leave His wondrous glory and suffer rejection, scorn, disrespect, misunderstanding, hatred, and humiliation for the sake of uniting with Himself those whose hearts were set against Him. The chosen sufferings of God are unmatched in meekness. He gave Himself to the worst to give us the best.

Because Thou didst thirst upon the tree
Thou art living water for me
I see Thy lips blistered and dry
Yet no need in thee to utter a why
Thy language transcended the fairest of quotes
The grandest of things wrote
Even a blood penned love note
Pales next to the pardon appeal from Thy dry throat
Does the Fountain of Life Himself thirst?
While the first Adam swallows a curse
And Judas kisses while holding a purse...
This is the glorious worst
Yet perfections work
The dying God thirsting that day
Is still crying for water today
Daily He waits as His cracking lips break

Taking His last minute to utter it is finished

Jesus quoted Psalm 22: "My God, my God, why have You forsaken me?" revealing that He was actually abandoned by God. Do you have any idea what this actually meant for Him? For all of eternity, God the Father has been united with the Son. The Trinity is completely inseparable, refusing to work without each other and having always been in and through and by and to each other. This was the only moment in time (and the only moment that will ever be) in which the Trinity was split up, the only time when Their perfect union was divided. The perfect sinless Christ, who had only ever known the atmosphere of heaven, took your rejection on Himself. Up to this point, He had only known the perfect presence of the Holy Spirit resting upon His obedience; but here, in this moment, He took on our disobedience and suffered abandonment by His Father. Of all things that He suffered, this was the most austere. He was rejected from the divine presence to restore you to the abiding presence.

Jesus, who received anything that He asked for, was blocked off from being heard: "O my God, I cry by day, but You do not answer, and by night, but I have no rest." The reason He can be the perfect giver of rest is because He suffered having no rest. The shame He endured was unfathomable, and until we see Him in His indescribable glory, we will never be able to understand one iota of the magnitude of His humiliation; "But I am a worm and not a man..." As Richard Rolle noted in his meditations on the passion: "He is despised and desecrated and...walks along completely naked under the gaze of everyone...naked as a worm, tortures surrounding you, and armed soldiers, the throng of people exceedingly thick and they are dragging You along with no respect."

God, the Creator and Sustainer of all things, allowed Himself to be disrespected and reduced to the value of an insect. Scripture states, "I am the scorn of men, and despised by the people." He who is adored by the angels was despised by humans. The hands that fashioned the earth were fastened with nails to the cross. He who sustains all creation with the breath of life allowed the soldiers to beat His life out of Him. His glorious diadem was replaced with a crown of thorns. The all-seeing one consented to be blindfolded.

> *A twisted crown of thorns too small in size*
> *Was pressed into His brow*
> *And blood flowed into His eyes*
> *Blinding Him to all but His prize*
> *His back is slashed open both deep and wide*
> *By whips made up of sin and pride*
> *This is humility personified*
> *The blood of God not realized*
> *And though men love things that are deified*
> *Not this God who is crucified*
> *But that is my God, He comes and dies.*

"All who see me laugh at me..." This moves me tremendously; I can't even begin to express how this breaks my heart and crushes my soul. There is nothing more holy, pure, glorious, and God-like than the suffering God-Man who — as He was being humiliated, disrespected, crushed, despised, rejected and hated — without one ounce of revenge, actually showed love and forgiveness to His torturers. Oh, Wisdom Divine, give us the true Spirit of Wisdom which cannot be understood by intellectual brilliance, but only by humility and selflessness; may we truly join You on the cross and demonstrate such wisdom to all the rebellious principalities of the air and all the rebellious sinners on the earth!

Oh precious blood of God, who loved me so
His hands are nailed and His head hangs low
His body is broken
His back is lashed open
The splintered cross is soaked in
blood, oh what love!
A love of me
I see His Glory when His feet upon the sea
But never such beauty
As when they're fastened to the tree
Your mocking crown
Separates your cross from the rest
And none can fathom God's sweet death
The breath of life
Breathing out His ghost
A dismayed angelic host
With the naked Christ upon the post
He's mostly – red
"Come down" they said
Man's faith is dead
But God bled
For sin to bring Adam in
Oh you bleed to set men free
You bled for my iniquity
Not Your cross for me
But my cross upon Thee

Appendix 1

A LETTER
TO MY IDENTITY
IN CHRIST BROTHERS

*"Now to the King eternal, immortal, invisible, the only
God, be honor and glory forever and ever."*
-1 Timothy 1:17 NASB

Brothers, I am afraid that we are in danger of eclipsing our dependency upon the experiential, abiding fellowship in Jesus with the truth concerning our identity in Him. It seems we have become so taken with what He has made us that we no longer recognize our desperate need of Him, not only in our teaching but also in our daily lives. I can hear Keith Green's timeless voice singing, "It's so hard to see when my eyes are on me." Is it possible that by looking so intently at who we are in Him, we have shifted our gaze from Him?

How do we endure in this life? Is it by looking at ourselves or by looking to Jesus? Richard Wurmbrand once said, "The 'I' must be abolished. 'I no longer live,' not the old Paul, not the new Paul, but Christ lives in me." In fact, the anthem of the new nature should be, "Worthy is the Lamb." Our identity in Christ is wrapped up in looking at Jesus in worship, depending upon Jesus and receiving from Him our daily bread, waiting and abiding with Him as submitted sons. The new nature recognizes that without Him we can do nothing and that we are helpless without Christ; such a mindset was impossible for the old nature, but now we are taught to recollect spiritual truths concerning our *selves*, that knowing the facts about what Christ has made *us* is the basis for victorious living.

Brothers, something is wrong when I am not taught to run into Jesus during times of difficulty but just to remind myself who I am. The Spiritual life does not stem from learning the facts about my new self, but rather forgetting about myself when I look at Him. Looking at my identity causes me to look away from Him. The new nature should be captivated by Him, by hearing His voice and experiencing His presence in daily life; the last thing the new nature will do is talk about itself, for even the Holy Spirit will not testify of Himself but only of the Son. As a matter of fact, our new outlook should be to overlook ourselves so that we might see Him. The only source of life is Jesus, and the perpetual gaze upon Him is the all-sufficient universal solution for everything in the life of a believer. Christ will not share the throne of your heart with you.

I am not saying that this wave is satanic or devilish but I am saying that it is dangerous because it reminds me of a distraction that took place before the beginning of time. Lucifer, "perfect and beautiful," was the handiwork of God; as an anointed angel, God placed him as ruler over the earth. But when he began to exalt what God made him to be, he crumbled; he began perfect, and self-focus was enough to disqualify him from the glory of God. Vance Havner said, "If Christ didn't come to save us from self infatuation, I don't know what the Savior came to do." He didn't save us from self-infatuation to bring us into a sanctified form of the same. David Popovici, one of the greatest men of God that I know who is currently giving his life to preach the gospel in hostile areas, once said to me, "It seems in the lives of many Christians that the self life is still king, he just changed his outfit." Michael Koulianos, founder of Jesus Image, taught on first love saying, "I never come out of prayer thinking how great I am, but rather I can't believe He wants me." This is the beauty of His love, not that we were worth something but that we were worth nothing, and He still died because He saw value in our worthlessness.

Even ministers I deeply respect are subtly shifting their focus. The other day, a minister that has greatly touched my life said, "When the I AM takes residence in you, you are able to say, "I am..." teaching that the evidence of God's presence is a revelation of self. This is askew: the evidence of the residence of the I AM is a life that proclaims, "HE IS." Moses' encounter with the I AM produced a greater dependency on God: "if You don't go with me, I don't go;" and when his face shone with glory, "he knew not." Gideon was called, "A mighty man of valor" simply because he didn't see himself as one. Paul wrote in 1 Corinthians 4:5, "We preach Christ, not ourselves..." A great man of God once told me, "Many people cannot recognize God's presence because they are too busy recognizing their own presence." There are many examples of this mentality in the midst of the Western church that I could point out, but rather let me just state what we need to see: Jesus is all. Anything that is preached or emphasized to pump us into frenzy about what we are in God is distorted identity. Pure identity in Christ is Christ. True identity in Christ is the exaltation and proclamation of Christ's great worth and glory.

After searching the Scriptures, I see that there is very little reference to self-awareness in the new life. We are not taught in Paul's letters a recollection practice any more than a doctor would tell a woman who wants to have children to remind herself she is pregnant. The only way to conceive the things that God wants to birth into the earth is to intimately experience Jesus. It is a life of coming unto Him that causes us to produce fruit.

In an intimate experience with my wife, the last thing I would do is confess to myself who I am: rather, I would allow myself to be captivated by her beauty and preoccupied with my desire for her. This is our identity—a people endlessly preoccupied with God Himself. Today I remembered this statement: "Men quickly fall in love with their own legacies." This statement seems to be truer among Christians than anywhere else. We claim to be driven to "make an impact," but the closer you draw to our hearts it seems to cover the lust for our own name and legacy. Our selfish humanity leads us to a hidden desire and a secret passion for our own personal significance. We constantly announce our activities, results and stories in our own ministries, but in reality we are just manifesting our Adamic pursuit for significance. I understand that the only way to tell people what is going on is to tell them what is going on, but it seems that under the guise of "identity in Christ" and "being fruitful," we have found a justification for exalting ourselves. Does our faith rest upon what we think ourselves to be in God, or are we content to remain nothing before God that He may show Himself strong? If this is accurate, this just indicates our failure to be wholly satisfied with His sweet presence in us, with just being His, and with loving Him and receiving His love everyday.

Appendix 2

COMMUNION WITH GOD

I have a friend named Harvey who is a very good man. His heart is kind, he loves Jesus and he desires deeply to please the Lord. Harvey has a prayer life, meaning; he makes time to sit with Jesus every day. One day I was teaching at a house group that the experiential presence of Jesus should not be a lottery but rather our source of life. Harvey came to me afterward and said, "Brother, I pray in the mornings and sometimes I sense His presence and others not so much. In fact if I were completely being honest, I would probably have to say that I barely ever experience His presence. But I pray and I read my Bible every day, for I am disciplined to do it. Are you suggesting that I can experience His presence every day?" To which I replied, "Not only can you, but you should."

God's presence should be our very life, the very source of our life, the animation of our life. Wherever His presence is not the center, life is not the center. Jesus is not a study time; He is a living individual, a person to be experienced. He is the life of life. If Christ is life, His presence is life. If Christ's presence is not in our life, there can be no life in our life. Without the presence of Jesus there is only death. Grip your Bible as hard as you wish, it is empty without His presence. Sing songs with every ounce of your being, but without His presence they have no life. Groups, services, evangelism, study, reading, praying, intercession, works, and anything else you can possible think of, are all dead without the presence of Jesus.

Many may say, "Well, you can't put any expectations on God. If you do, you will set yourself up for frustration and failure." Friend, isn't it putting an expectation on my wife to be there when I meet with her? Is it foolish to suggest that the presence of my wife has vision, touch, hearing and energy? The sun it is only a ball of fire millions of miles away and it shines down, illuminates my day, warms my skin, and changes my complexion. The Godhead is much more than this and He has made His abode in us. The internal confluence of the Spirit is the influence of God in His people. Now I am not suggesting that there should be physical sensation every moment of everyday. I am speaking of something far more valuable than external feelings, I am talking about the internal bliss of His presence. There is a major difference between a massage and the presence of a loved one. Both are felt, but one is much better than the other. Ask anyone who has lost someone, more than an endless massage, they desire just one second of the presence of their loved one. The internal bliss of His nearness is heaven on the earth and is the source of our endurance and victory in this present life.

I once had an interesting conversation with a dear friend who was having major issues in his marriage. After the long list of all the things she was and wasn't doing, he said, "I would divorce her if it wasn't so clearly a sin in the Scriptures. I guess that is what marriage is: holding on to the Word of God over your feelings." I immediately counted how many times during that very conversation I had thought of how badly I wanted to get home to hang out with my wife. The kids were in bed and nighttime is the time that we have nothing to do but simply be together. It is one of my favorite times of the day.

If you notice, I just laid out two very different husbands. The first one feels that life is all about gritting your teeth and clinching to the plain text of the word so as to not transgress it. The second is consumed by a lover's blissful attraction, anticipation, and desire. Herein is the difference between the spirit of religion and the Spirit of God.

God wants to be fellowshipped with and sweetly experienced. He is not a cold, dead, penned-out requirement upon your life that must be adhered to in order to escape His wrath. Even if you could obey the letter by yourself it still wouldn't qualify you for eternal life, because eternal life is the experiential life that flows from Him. To quote A.B. Simpson, "it is more a Son issue than a sin issue." Not to mention, sin is eradicated by God's presence. For the burning fires of our passions are put out by the rain of His presence.

Eternal life is union and intimate relationship with God, not the final reward for following all the rules. For the most part this is how people approach prayer. They say to themselves, "I am going to go in there to read and pray if it is the last thing I do!" This shows a lack of experiential fellowship which says instead, "There is nothing in this world I would rather do than to rest upon His breast and access the divine treasure chest." Just because it hasn't been your experience up until this point doesn't mean that it cannot be or that it is not supposed to be. As a matter of fact, as we make the presence of the Lord the center of our life and we choose to live our lives through the animation that comes from Him, we will see amazing results: love for Him and others springing up and covering every corner of our hearts; marvelous joy in the midst of our trials planted deep inside of our being to overcome even in the mundane; peace beyond understanding that permeates our minds and produces patience in all circumstances, goodness and kindness to others, faithfulness in our lives, gentleness in speech and action, and self control in all things. Our relationship with Christ is no less experiential than our initial encounter with Him; life in the Spirit is no less experiential than the day you were first filled with the Spirit. My friends, experiencing God is Christianity. Experiencing Him is not an option or a lottery; it is the source of our life.

So with all of this experience talk, what can we expect to experience when we pray? Let us look at how Jesus spoke of encountering Him:

"If anyone is thirsty, let him come to Me and drink. He who believes in Me, as the Scripture said, 'From his innermost being will flow rivers of living water.'" But this He spoke of the Spirit, whom those who believed in Him were to receive."

John 7:37-39

"Come to me" - if there is an issue in experiencing Jesus the problem is in the coming. What does it mean to "come to Jesus"? First of all it means, leaving everything else behind, both your failures and your victories. It means leaving your own way and coming to *Him*. It does not mean coming to your Bible, your iPod or your service. Coming to Jesus means that you come to the living person. It means looking unto Him and giving Him all of our attention. It is adoration. As I look unto Him with all my attention in adoration, removing and refusing all other thoughts, I begin to be drawn to Him. He is like an immense magnetic force that focuses all your desires toward Himself to the degree that they are not obstructed by or directed toward something else. To come to Him means to give Him your complete attention leaving all else behind and adoring Him. I repeat: if there is an issue, it is right here. The experience of God is so rare because scattered minds are so common, and if adoration is not the center, we are not pursuing God but something else. God simply will not work with this. Even Isaac (representing all the promises that God has made you) will not be tolerated in that place that belongs only to God. If I know anything I know this: every one of my failures was initially a failure to come to Him.

Who can drink? Anyone who will come to Him can imbibe. You must realize that the drinking of the Lord is not restricted to anyone, but is given freely to any who will simply come.

What does it mean to drink? It means that all of your inward thirsts are quenched by God. The inward thirsts are all those things that the soul of man constantly craves, the innate burning lust for things with which to satisfy itself. When we come to Him, we can expect that His presence (because we have come to Him) will satisfy our souls. His presence will quench every thirst. If you have a problem with any lust, not just sexual but any kind of longing whatsoever, His presence will quench it for He is the living water. So let us come to Him to drink.

Jesus shows us that the initial drink becomes an endless drinking when He causes the rivers of living water to flow on the inside of us. We can expect to not only be filled but to be able to drink our fill from this confluence on the inside of us. That is the image that Jesus gives to us of a life that receives the Spirit: an endless well of fellowship that quenches your cravings. Jesus states in John 4:14, "but whoever drinks of the water that I will give him shall never thirst; but the water that I will give him will become in him a well of water springing up to eternal life." No wonder holiness is the fruit of being addicted to the maximum pleasure of life, which is God Himself. We must drink. No amount of outward contact with the river will quench the inward thirst of the soul. You must come to Him yourself and not just be around individuals who have water themselves.

What else can we expect when we come to Him?

Isaiah 26:3 says, "*He will keep him in perfect peace whose mind is stayed on Him.*" You can expect the turbulence of the soul be stilled by His presence. As we look to Him and give Him our attention we are placed in perfect peace.

Psalm 16:11 says, "*In the presence of the Lord is fullness of joy...and pleasure forever more.*" We can expect pleasure and fullness of joy. I know so many people would love to take this verse out of the Scriptures because then they wouldn't have such a scandal in their lives when they claim they are in His presence yet have no experience of it.

In John 6:35, 57 we see that the Lord will dispense into us the Bread of Life, that revelation of the Word that feeds our souls; just as natural food animates and energizes us, this spiritual food will be our animation and life source. Most Christians walk around with their Bibles like a culinary student with his cookbook. They stand around exchanging recipes and showing each other pictures of the best dishes, but no amount of recipes can actually feed you. If you give a starving man a cookbook he will die. This book of recipes must become a delectable spread and that is the activity of the presence of the Spirit: He breathes upon the word and makes it actual nourishment to our souls. You can expect God to fill you and animate you with His own Life Bread: "As the living Father sent Me, and I live because of the Father, so he who eats Me, he also will live because of Me." "Jesus said to them, 'I am the bread of life; he who comes to Me will not hunger.'" The famine of the Word of the Lord is simply a generation that will not come to Him.₁

We can expect the light of His face for 1 John 1:3 equates light with fellowship. Light illuminates. You can expect clarity, vision and the shining radiance of His face. "...if we walk in the light...we have fellowship with one another."

To recap, what can we expect when we come to Him for Himself alone every day?

We can expect the quenching of our thirst and the refreshing of our souls through the living water.

We can expect the satisfaction and filling of our soul through the Bread of Life/Word/Presence.

We can expect the illumination of His light on our lives, ways, and minds.

We can expect real fullness of joy to be poured into us as the strength of our lives.

We can expect a pleasure that is even deeper than ordinary satisfaction, and receive the bliss of heaven here and now in the person of the Spirit.

We can expect peace beyond what can be understood.

So let us come to Him daily and thereby enter into the bliss of His person and live by the animation and empowerment of God's presence in the earth today; THE HOLY SPIRIT.

---

1 Amos 8:11

Into The Cloud

144

SPIRITUAL MAXIMS

The reason why many people fall asleep in silent prayer is because they have sadly taught themselves that life is united with noise.

It is through fellowship that we enjoy the riches of divine life.
-Witness Lee

It is necessary that God be feared as Lord, honored as Father, so that he may be loved as spouse.
-Bernard of Clairvaux

Break into the earth as much revelation as you can, and if you are plagiarized by someone, they become servant to your eternal reward.

To be plagiarized is to have your eternal reward stored up by another.

The Father sees in secret. If we neglect the secret place we will hear the same words God said in the garden "Adam, where are you?"

Be careful not to ask Christ, "what would you have me do?" before "who are you Lord?"

Solitude is ridding yourself of the external noise while stillness is ridding yourself of the internal noise-so that you can hear Him.

Tis divine life alone that maketh life divine.

When you recognize how important it is to abide in his presence you recognize how evil it's obstructions are.

Never let an opportunity to make money trump a direct word from The Lord or after the money is gone you will still be paying for it.

As we translate the glory we've seen we can transfer it for others to see.

Revelation is a means by which we can transfer the glory current.

It is in the prophets personal revelation of God that he receives God's communication to the world.

His presence is the greatest miracle.

Walking in the a Spirit is yielding into the influence of the internal confluence.

The "abiding presence" is not just a theological truth but a sustained manifestation of Him on the inside of us.

I am convinced that difficulty in life and prayer are in exact proportion to the attention that we give to our self life.

I believe that Christians should here within themselves the endless melody of Christ, "Come away, come away with me my love."

In John 10:9-10, Jesus connects our abundant life with eating in Him. Abundant life is contingent upon consumption of Him.

The phrase "follow me" is a command to fix your gaze upon Him and remain in His presence.

"Because thou didst thirst upon the tree, Thou art living water for me."

Waiting is not the postponing of your initiative but rather the death of it.

Men have always use the written word to discredit the present acting Christ.
-See John 7:52

We must redefine the word evil. Evil is everything out of rhythm with God.

Your life is in your looking.
-See Isaiah 45:22

Jesus refused to act outside of the empowerment of spiritually perceiving God's desires.

The fact that John 5:38 is right before John 5:39 reveals to us that the Word is more than the Scriptures.

Moses had Aaron and Hur to uphold his hands for the salvation of Israel. But Thou hath none to hold thy hands but nails alone.

We are never commanded to make people honor us but rather to honor one another.

The more you come to know Christ the more you will experience Him.
-See 2 Peter 1:2

My dad used to tell me, "it is more honorable to honor a dishonorable man than it is honorable to honor an honorable man."

Amnesia of His mercy is the cause of judgment of your brother.

Why must I repent? So that Christ might been made manifest in me.

The primary purpose for repentance is for the manifestation of Christ. The reason for repentance is because Christ is not manifest.

Anxiety is the seed of Atheism.
-Unknown

There is an inseparable union between the manifestation of Christ and repentance.
-See John 1:31

The Son descends from heaven to our level, and ascends back to heaven bringing us up with Him to the divine level.
-Dr. Raymond E. Brown

If the word of the Lord is of no significance to you than you are still in darkness.

Frequency of stillness increases facility in stillness and also longevity of stillness.

Some gifts are free, others you must qualify for. You must past the test.
-Tony Kemp

A man is born again by inhaling Christ's exhale on the cross.

To the degree that we recognize our helplessness we will look unto Jesus.

"...the world did not know Him." There is the definition of "The World" - has no relationship with Jesus.

Do for other people what you would like them to do for you, regardless if they do it for you or not. It makes Jesus smile on your life.

Be careful that you don't look down on preaching, for when it is touched by the Spirit, it is the dispensing of God into your soul.

Even after the branches are connected to the vine the branches are still dependent upon the vine.

As you see Him, you begin to see things through Him.
—Michael Koulianos

When the word of the Lord comes into the heart intercession bursts out of the heart.

"Frozen in His sweetness" is when the stillness we offer Him is swallowed by the stillness that comes from Him.

Remember the prisoners, as though in prison with them, and those who are ill-treated, since you yourselves also are in the body.

You can come to your bible without coming to The Lord but it is difficult to come to The Lord without coming to your bible.
-Witness Lee

See to it that you do not refuse Him who is speaking.
-Hebrews 12:25

There is a major difference between life experience and the experience of Life.

Honestly, do you live by a continuous revelation of Jesus?

The edibility of the heavenly Scroll reveals that the Scriptures are not confined to the lesson of the letter.

God's speech must be an excessive speech because it comes from the immensity of The Divine Nature.
-Meister Eckhart

"...as The Lord directed me."
-Jeremiah

His rule, His love and His life are all in the gospel.

If adoration is not center, I am.

There is no better route to or practice of oneness than eat my body.
See John 6:57, Matt 26:26

This is why I live, to need you and to continually lay my life at Your feet and worship You. I am Yours, save me.

The Pharisees only knew what God had said but Jesus knew what God was saying.

Friend your not bad you're dead.
-Leonard Ravenhill

"Doctrine can be a wind to blow believers away from the Head and from the body."
-Witness Lee

"He wasn't the greatest preacher I ever heard but he had intimacy with God like no one else."
-Ravenhill on Tozer

His friends are aware of His plans and hear His voice.
-John 15:15

Sometimes as I read the Scriptures, I feel as if these pages are breathing.

If you are lacking peace and joy, then the rule of the King is somewhere compromised in your heart.

Experiential union has its roots in experiential fellowship.

Someone once asked me, "do you really experience His presence every time you pray?" Absolutely, without His presence it's not communion.

Nothing will so disturb your gaze upon Him as turning your attention to you.

Knowing your identity vs experiential intimacy-you can tell yourself you're pregnant a million times but only intimacy can make it a reality

Cain gave his best but God wanted blood.

How do you kill fear? Seeing Him who is unseen.
-See Hebrews 11

For many believers today, the self life is still king, he just changed his outfit.
-David Popovici

I bet the Roman soldiers didn't know that every laceration they gave to Christ was renting the veil to God.

The evidence that the "I AM" is in us is that we have become a "He is."

Have we forgotten how to lay our head on His chest? Or does the nothingness of it irritate our active souls?

If someone doesn't walk in integrity out in the world there is no way they are walking in integrity alone in their home.

The writer of Hebrews writes to them, "you have BECOME dull of hearing."

Obedience is when an individual's life is yielded to the extent that God can perform through that man the things He has spoken to him.

What you win them with is what you win them to.
-J.I. Packer

We were not created with the capacity to fathom the triune God, but we were created with the ability to receive Him.
-Witness Lee

Pride is the fortress of demons, the source of hard heartedness, a sign of barrenness and the foe of God.
-John Climacus

Pride is the custodian of sin.
-John Climacus

Did you know that it is an evil thing to not drink from the Fountain of Living Water?
-See Jeremiah 2:13

Do you want to slip away from God? Pay mild attention to Him.
-See Hebrews 2:1

We live by Him through enjoying Him.
-Witness Lee

The Lord laid this into me this morning... "do not waste time on those who are not serious."

Don't play games with God and don't play into the games of others.

The reward of seeking God is God. To not seek Him is to not value Him.
-Daniel Kolenda

If God's presence is not at every point necessary, than there is a part of this walk that God wants us to fulfill apart from Him.

I think God is repulsed by the heart that thinks, teaches or believes that we can make it through suffering without His presence.

The border to eternity is not ahead of us but runs parallel to us and we can cross over at any time.
-Bonnke

Oh scattered soul, you have locked the gates into the presence of God.

It seems whatever book of the bible I am reading all I can see is our need of His presence.

I found sin overcoming me and temptation too strong to resist. I went to God and He whispered, "Christ in you!"
-A.B. Simpson

Just like marriage there are certain things Jesus will only do to you when you are alone with Him.

"Remember Jesus Christ..."
-2 Timothy 2:8

"Oh that my people would listen to Me..."
-God, Psalm 81:13

I had to learn to take my spiritual life from Jesus every moment, to breathe Himself and as I breathed myself out.
-A.B. Simpson

Even if you could obey Christ on your own it would not please God because He is only pleased with His Son. Christ must be our obedience.
-Witness Lee

The maturity of the Life we posses is dependent upon the continuous reception of that same Life.
-Witness Lee

The kingdom is The Lord among us and with us.
-Witness Lee

We must seek to find Christ present in the scriptures not merely as type and shadow but as the living word, the present speaking of God.

Self exaltation is rebellion against God. Rebellion against God is self exaltation.

My heart desires nothing so much as it desires to desire you.
-William of St. Thierry

Let this penetrate. Lucifer could no longer glorify God because he magnified what God made him.

The prophet has become his message. He does not prepare messages, he speaks what has been spoken into him; he speaks what he himself has become.

Love is repaid by love alone
-St. John of the Cross

The body, humbled by fasting, begins to pass from habits to the spontaneous service of the Spirit.
-William of St. Thierry

Three things that infiltrate and erode covenant relationships: jealousy, envy and competition.

If you don't enjoy and express God in this life, what makes you think you will in the next?
–David Popovici

In adoration of Christ we open the valve of receptivity.

There is no level of maturity in God in which we are exempt from the need to be led by the Spirit.

When I am afraid, I put my trust in you.
-Psalm 56:3

It is vanity to love what passes quickly and not to look ahead where eternal joy abides.
-Thomas Kempis

Whoever wishes to understand fully the words of Christ must pattern his whole life on that of Christ.
-Thomas Kempis

"Stillness is the mother of prayer."
-Greek Orthodox proverb

"Not a God hath wounds but Thou alone."
-John Stott

"The mystic is the person who is seeking to find God in a deeper and more transformative way."
-Bernard McGinn

"We are nothing and if ever we think otherwise, we have entered deception."
-See Galatians 6:3

Missions exists because worship doesn't.
-John Piper

The prophet is the one with whom God can share His ecstasy and His agony.
-David Popovici

If you'll wait, He'll listen.
-See Psalm 40:1

True Spirituality is the subjection of the will to God.
-Zac Poonen

One of the greatest deceptions of our time is that knowledge is spirituality.
-Zac Poonen

Another one of the greatest deceptions of our time is that excitement is spirituality.
-Zac Poonen

"God became man that He might dispense Himself into men."
-Witness Lee

A woman in marital issues once prayed, "God I want to honor you through my life!" To which God replied, "then start honoring your husband."

That man who loves to voice the things he has given up for God, has yet to truly count those things rubbish for the sake of knowing Jesus.

Beware of anyone who sacrifices Isaac in public. For these are private matters between the heart of God and the heart of man.

Trust is the release of self unto God.

"Eric, why are you so quiet?" I replied with a smile but in my heart I said, "I can't find the right enough motive to speak."
-Journal-2003

Humility waits.

Only after the hose is fastened to the Spicket can the Spicket release water into the hose. Jesus said, "remain in me and I in you."

Have you ever connected anxiety and pride?
-See 1 Peter 5:6-7

The only garment permitted to enter into the castle of Grace is humility.

When you clothe yourself with humility God will clothe you with grace.
-See 1 Peter 5:5

*The spiritual man is the one whom the Holy Spirit wears like a
mantle.*
-William of St. Thierry (The Golden Letter)

Do not spend time talking with those who love to find fault in others.
-Maximus the Confessor

*Stillness of spirit is an endless worship of God and a standing in the
very Presence.*
-John Climacus

It is not wrong to look for a door but it is wrong to make a door.

Only the captive are joyless.

One need not say much to pray well.
-St. John Vianney

The still voice is heard in stillness.

Nothing is so opposed to God as self-sufficiency.
-Madame Guyon

*Choosing to drink the Wine of Heaven will make us wine for the
earth.*

*The obstructions to seeing God are all those things that we give
attention to that are not His direct presence.*

*Jesus forever destroyed the gap between the mountaintop and the
valley by bringing the mountaintop into the valley.*

*Men are uncomfortable in silence because we have sadly taught
ourselves that life is united with noise.*

We're alive because we ate Him but we live by eating Him.

God is not after your efforts near as much as He is after your heart.

It seems that the one of the greatest diseases in the midst of Christianity is self-effort. It is "might" and "power" that so often obstructs His Spirit.

Abiding in Christ is as simple as breathing and just as crucial.

The greatest problem with the fall is that we no longer knew His abiding presence. The coming of the Spirit changed all this forever.
-Gordon Fee

Presence is a delicious word-because it points to one of our truly great gifts. Nothing else can take the place of presence.
-Gordon Fee

We are much more likely to inquire than to adore.
-A.W. Tozer

God's Kingdom is established upon, empowered by and administrated through His own speaking.

He who will not use the thoughts of other men's brains proves that he has no brains of his own.
-Charles Spurgeon

He who never reads will never be read.
-Charles Spurgeon

It is idolatry to allow another to influence your paradigm more than the Scriptures themselves.

Self can only be expelled by Spiritual experience.
-A.W. Tozer

When we obey we express the nature of the One we are being obedient to.
-Michael Dow

Jesus says in John 14:12, "Verily, verily..." because He knew this was something mankind was sure to doubt.
-A.B. Simpson

The root of all neglect of the secret place is self-sufficiency.

Be assured that frustration is the only outcome for plans that do not originate in God.

Prophecy is far more about the feelings of God than the future of man.

If you are not dependent, you are His enemy.
-Hanna Ben-Haim *(said to me in the wilderness in which Jesus fasted 40 days)*

Are you content to follow Jesus afar off? Can you contemplate suspended communion with Christ without alarm? Can you bear to have your Beloved walking contrary to you, because you walk contrary to Him?
-Charles Spurgeon

His wounds are His wisdom.

Two ways to cause the grace of God to wane in your life: 1. Don't listen to what God has said 2. Don't listen for what God is saying.

Without His presence our devotion is only external.

In other religions prayer is a requirement but in Christ prayer is an invitation.

We despise waiting on God in exact proportion to our selfish ambition.

I would rather work along side one man with humility in his heart than ten miracle workers without it.

If we go on apart from His presence it means that we value whatever it is that we are doing more than we value Him.

When the eyes of the soul looking out meet the eyes of God looking in, heaven has begun right here on earth.
-A.W. Tozer

Lack of joy is a sign of spiritual fatigue.

SONSHIP
INTERNATIONAL

ABOUT THE AUTHOR

I met Jesus the first day that I saw Evangelist Steve Hill at Brownsville Assembly of God in Pensacola, Florida in 1996. His face was radiating with light and for the first time in my life, Jesus was manifest to me in the preaching of the cross in the power of the Spirit. I have not been the same since.

I graduated the Brownsville Revival School of Ministry in 2001 then returned to FIRE school of ministry to enter Dr. Michael L. Brown's mentoring group in 2002. In 2003 I started working at Christ for all Nations, the ministry of Reinhard Bonnke. I was married in 2004 to Brooke, the love of my life and my best friend. Today we have two girls, Madison Tate and Lia Ashlyn.

I was laid off at Christ for all Nations in 2007 and started working construction till God spoke deep into my being in summer of 2010. He said, "I want you to be my spokesman." I knew in that moment everything would change. He was requiring absolute faith. After a two weeks notice, I quit working construction and started giving my life to the gospel alone.

Since that day God has been gracious to back His gospel with signs, wonders and miracles. Cancers, Hepatitis, broken bones, ADHD and many more sicknesses have been healed by the power of Christ's blood. We have witnessed hundreds surrender their lives to Jesus in response to the gospel.

Dear reader, we are under a mandate from the Lord to set the captives free by the foolishness of the cross preached in the power of the Spirit. For the gospel is the offering of God's presence to men. God has crystalized the ministry of my life under Sonship International to bring the church into a deeper awareness, consciousness and experience of God's presence in their daily lives. This is why we live and breath in the earth, to aid men in experiential fellowship with God, by the presence of the Spirit and the perpetual revelation of Jesus Christ. God has graced us to bring the church into a life of both enjoying Christ and being animated by Him. Those that are led by the Spirit are the sons of God. SONSHIP!

ORDER NOW

UNION
The Thirsting Soul Satisfied In God
AMAZON, NOOK, KINDLE and iBOOKS

BURN

Melting Into The Image of Jesus
AMAZON, NOOK, KINDLE and iBOOKS

NOTES

NOTES

<u>NOTES</u>

CPSIA information can be obtained at www.ICGtesting.com
Printed in the USA
BVOW03s1632180515

400229BV00004B/5/P